GW00360162

Old Holborn

GROW YOUR OWN

Written by George Seddon

WINDWARD

Executive Managers	Kelly Flynn
	Susan Egerton-Jones
Designer	Sheila Volpe
Editor	Rachel Grenfell
Production	Peter Phillips

Edited and designed by the Artists House Division of
Mitchell Beazley International Ltd
Artists House
14–15 Manette Street
London W1V 5LB
In conjunction with Old Holborn

This edition published 1987 by
WINDWARD
an imprint owned by W. H. Smith & Son Limited
Registered No 237811 England Trading as
WHS Distributors
St John's House East Street, Leicester LE1 6NE

"An Artists House Book"
© Mitchell Beazley Publishers 1981 and 1987
© Text George Seddon 1987 (excluding recipes)

The recipes in this book were originally created by
Helena Radecka

ISBN 0 7112 0491 8

Typeset by Bookworm Typesetting, Manchester
Printed in Hong Kong by
Mandarin Offset

Foreword

You will not find the word "Asphodel" in this book or phrases like "the gleaming golden patina of the sun enhanced dandelion". There are no frills, fancies and furbelows. This book is a rarity. It is full of stark useful facts. Here is contained the A–Z of vegetable gardening in plain, sensible, easily understood prose.

I have read a gardening book which explained in detail how the owner of the garden invited his guests according to their gardening skills, and how instead of libations of manure being fed to the plants, libations of gin were fed to his gardening slaves who then turned his sods and sowed his seeds for him, albeit in somewhat crooked rows!

Here you are not entertained, you are instructed. And I have never seen the procedures of gardening from the structure of the soil to the more subtle art of the growing of an aubergine more explicitly explained.

Then, having grown your vegetables, Mr Seddon explains how to deal with their well being, how to eradicate their diseases and how to harvest them too. The commercial grower needs to harvest his crop as fully grown as possible, but you, the keen amateur, will harvest your produce when it is young and succulent and ambrosial.

After the harvest; you will find in the book recipes for your produce, some of them splendidly novel ways of serving up your vegetables, which will make you realise that all your toil has been worthwhile.

There is one tip I can pass on from my grandfather not contained in this excellent *Old Holborn Grow Your Own* book. When his first broad beans began to flower, he would pinch off the top three inches of the plants to prevent blackfly infestation. He then washed the cuttings and my grandmother cooked them briefly, as you would cabbage ... Here then was a delicious vegetable tasting of broad bean.

CYRIL FLETCHER   3

Contents

INTRODUCTION

Great changes have occurred in vegetable growing over the past decade. There are changes in the ways in which they are grown, in the reasons for growing them, and in the choice of what is grown.

Science has to be thanked for the changes in the methods of cultivation since some, although by no means all, of the extensive research into commercial vegetable crops has also benefited the ordinary gardener. One of the main findings is that many vegetables can be grown much closer together than was recommended in the past. Individual vegetables may be smaller, but the yield from the same amount of ground will probably be higher.

This coincides with a change in our tastes. Today, we prefer our vegetables smaller, younger and more tender. Size is out; succulence is in. In contrast, during the last great surge of domestic vegetable growing in the 1970s, when bad harvests and high inflation made shop prices soar, we grew our own produce mainly to beat scarcity and save money.

Scarcity is no longer the problem, especially in towns, where supermarket shelves are overflowing with vegetables from all over the world and therefore permanently in season. These same supermarkets have given us a taste for a wider range of vegetables. Many may have been imported by air 'for freshness', as they claim, but only if we raise our own vegetables and cook them freshly gathered, will we appreciate their true flavour, retain most of the nutrients and cut the cost of indulging in out-of-the-ordinary produce. This, and the pleasure of growing what we eat and eating what we grow, is reason enough for cultivating a kitchen garden.

THE BASICS

GARDEN SOILS

People do not usually choose a house because of the texture of the soil in the garden, even though it will be of vital importance to the gardener. Only the local climate will have a greater influence on what can be grown. Nothing can be done to change the climate, although growing under glass can give vulnerable crops protection from the cold. The structure of the soil can be changed to some extent, but the task may be arduous.

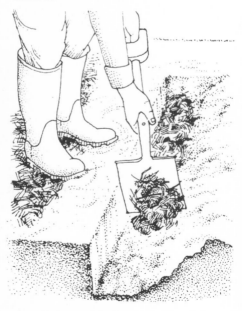

A spade is one of the four essential tools for cultivating the garden. Always keep a straight spade. If you dig at an angle you will have to push the spade just as far into the soil, but you will not dig as deep.

A fork, rather than a spade, is used to turn over heavy or stony soil, for shallow cultivation of the surface and for lifting root crops.

The main types of garden soil are sandy, clay, loamy, chalky, and, to a lesser extent, peaty. The texture of a soil – before the gardener gets to work on it – depends on the size of the particles of the rock from which the soil was originally formed. For example, sand particles are comparatively large, varying between 0.02 and 2mm, while clay particles are less than 0.002mm. Silt (mud) particles are somewhere in between.

Sandy soil. This is the lightest soil – more than 75 per cent is sand particles. Although it is easy to work and warms up quickly in spring, it is so well drained that the nutrients are soon washed out. Also, it is a 'hungry' soil, needing continuous feeding with compost or manure to build up humus. (Humus,

7

A Dutch hoe is used to kill young weeds by slicing them just below the surface of the soil and leaving them to die.

the complicated substance which gives the soil fertility, is present as minute, black, amorphous particles or as a jelly-like coating of the sand, silt and clay particles.) With added humus, peas and beans, cauliflowers and potatoes will crop well on sandy soil.

Clay soil. This is the heaviest soil, with at least 75 per cent of clay and silt particles. It is cold and poor draining, sticky if wet, like rock when dry. It needs massive additions of compost, manure and peat, and also some lime, to produce a more open, free draining, warmer and less acid soil. Improved in this way, clay soil will grow good crops of most vegetables, with the exception of roots.

Peaty soil. This is acid, badly draining and short of nutrients. It needs liming and draining to break down the raw peat into humus. When well cultivated, it will grow good crops of potatoes, celery and onions.

A rake is invaluable for breaking the soil to a fine tilth and for removing stones and rubbish from the surface.

Loamy soil. If you have this type of soil, you are lucky indeed. Loamy soils have more sand than clay particles, plus a lot of organic matter. Reasonably warm, and easy to dig, they hold moisture without becoming waterlogged and the plant nutrients are not readily washed out. If a high level of humus is maintained with manure or compost, such a soil is ideal.

Chalky soil. There are two problems. The soil may be too alkaline for many vegetables. Also, the calcium carbonate and calcium bicarbonate in the soil combine with other important elements, making them unavailable to the plants. To counteract excess lime add compost, manure and peat in large quantities. Brassicas, peas and beans should then do particularly well, but do not try to grow potatoes.

WHAT PLANTS LIVE ON

The plant takes up through its roots various elements in the soil. These are the raw materials from which, with the help of sunlight and oxygen and carbon dioxide in the air, the plant processes its foods. The three most important elements are:

Nitrogen is important for growth of leaves and stems. It is made available to plants by soil bacteria, which convert ammonia and nitrite into nitrate.

Phosphorus is vital for a good root system and seed production.

Potassium helps to make plants more resistant to disease.

Other elements needed for a balanced diet, but in smaller quantities, include magnesium and sulphur and several 'trace' elements. If the soil is lacking in these they have to be added, or the plants will suffer.

Normally, the elements a plant takes out of the soil are replaced when the plant dies. If, however, we dig up vegetables, the elements must be replaced by feeding the soil with either compost or manure (now scarce). Compost is made, with little trouble and no expense, from all the vegetable waste from the kitchen and garden.

To make good compost, build a box from loose boards held in place by a wooden frame. Leave gaps between the boards to let in some air, but take care – if the gaps are too big, too much heat will escape from the decaying vegetation. Build up the heap inside the box with 6-8in (15-20cm) layers of vegetable waste. As you build it, sprinkle a little sulphate of ammonia over alternate layers and a little lime over the intervening layers. Spray each layer with water. Cover the top with 1in (2.5cm) of soil and put a plastic cover on top to keep out the rain.

Properly made spring waste should be compost by summer, summer waste by autumn, and autumn waste by spring.

Compost or manure both feed the soil and improve its texture. Fertilizers just feed.

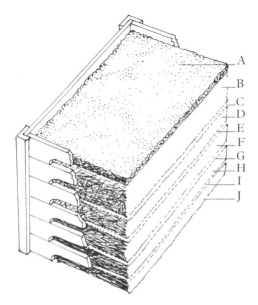

A Soil; B Vegetable waste; C Sulphate of ammonia or farmyard manure; D Vegetable waste; E Lime; F Vegetable waste; G Sulphate of ammonia or farmyard manure; H Vegetable waste; I Lime; J Vegetable waste.

Organic fertilizers include bone meal, fish meal, dried blood and seaweed meal. Inorganic fertilizers are made from chemicals. Although they produce quick results, there is no lasting improvement in the soil.

What we call 'the soil' is made up of far more than ground-down rock, minerals and decayed vegetable matter. Half of its volume is air and water. Then there are the bacteria in their millions, most of them beneficial and essential, although there are some exceptions. There are also fungi – some good, some bad. Moving up the size scale there are mites, eelworms, springtails, worms (invaluable for aerating the soil), beetles (some 1,300 species), centipedes (good), millipedes (bad), earwigs, slugs and snails. These are but some of the inhabitants of the soil.

SOWING UNDER GLASS

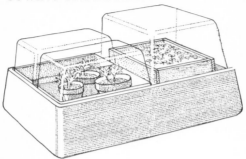

Except in very warm areas, early crops can be grown only if they are protected in some way from the cold. Even though seeds may withstand frost, they will not germinate below a certain temperature, which varies from plant to plant. Sowing in a greenhouse, frame or under cloches can begin weeks before sowing outdoors. Indoors, a heated propagator can be used.

Seeds are sown in seed compost in pots or trays. Or, in order to avoid root disturbance later, peat blocks can be used. Two or three seeds are sown in each block; the strongest seedling is saved and is planted out in the block itself.

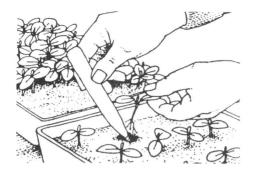

Seedlings sown in trays or ordinary pots are pricked out when large enough to handle, to give them room to grow. Hold the seedlings by their seed leaves (the first to appear) and not by their stems.

The day before planting out, water the seedlings in their pots or trays. When planting them in the garden, disturb the roots as little as you can by lifting them with as big a ball of compost as possible. Lower them into holes, at the recommended distances, using a trowel or dibber. Plants which have been grown in single pots or peat blocks suffer the least disturbance and will forge ahead of the others. Firm the soil around the transplanted plants before watering.

SOWING OUTDOORS

The first three stages in growing plants outdoors are (1) sowing the seeds in drills; (2) germination, which may occur after only a few days, but can take up to two or three weeks, and (3) the first thinning of the seedlings to prevent overcrowding.

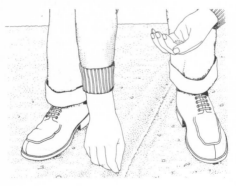

Seeds are of all sizes and sowing the small ones can be tricky. Do not try to sow them straight from the packet – they are likely to come out in a sudden rush. Empty a few into the palm of one hand, then take a small pinch of them and sow thinly along the row; the more thinly you sow the seeds, the less thinning will be required later.

Larger seeds are far easier. Peas and French and runner beans can easily be spaced out along the drills. In case some seeds fail to germinate, it is wise to sow a few extra at the end of the row, to fill any gaps. Broad beans are often sown without drills, by making a hole for each bean with a dibber.

Some large seeds are sown in groups of two or three along the row. In thinning, only the strongest seedling of the group is kept. Beets are a special case; their 'seeds' are in fact a little cluster of seeds and thinning is done by removing all but the strongest seedling.

The problem of small vegetable seeds can be overcome in some cases by buying pelleted seeds, which are more expensive, but the range is not as extensive as with flower seeds. The seeds have been given a coating of soil/clay to make them large enough to handle. The soil or compost in which they are sown must be moist enough to soften the coating but not too wet. Nor must the soil be allowed to dry out after sowing.

PROTECTING THE CROPS

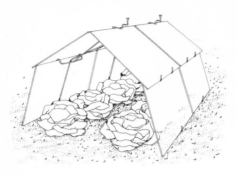

Cloches add weeks to the vegetable gardening year. In early spring, cover the ground where seeds are to be sown to warm up the soil, and keep the cloches in place over the young plants until the warm weather comes. In autumn, put cloches over late-sown crops to save them from the first frosts.

Heated frames are a cheaper alternative to a greenhouse. Unheated they are invaluable during the critical stage of hardening off indoor-grown seedlings before they go out into the garden.

ROTATING THE CROPS

The vegetable garden is usually divided into three parts. Each part is devoted for one year to one of the three main groups of vegetables – peas and beans, plus onions; the brassicas; and roots. Each year one group is moved to the ground occupied by another in the previous year. The reason is twofold: to provide each group with nutrients and to prevent the build-up of disease which would be inevitable if the same crops were grown in the same ground year after year. This diagram shows how crop rotation works.

FIRST YEAR	SECOND YEAR
Grow peas, beans, onions, leeks, shallots, lettuce, endive, celery, radishes. These vegetables need a rich soil, so their part of the garden is given heavy dressings of manure or compost. Do not lime. The vegetables in this group move on the following year to ground in which the brassicas were grown.	Grow cabbages, Brussels sprouts, cauliflowers, savoys, broccoli, kale, turnips, swedes, kohlrabi, spinach. Brassicas are given lime, which helps to combat club root. Fertilizer can also be applied, but not manure. The following year the brassicas move to where the roots were grown.

THIRD YEAR
Grow carrots, beetroots, parsnips, celeriac, potatoes. (If many potatoes are grown the garden could be divided into four parts, one just for potatoes. The cycle would then be spread over four years, peas and beans following the potatoes.) Give roots a general fertilizer, but no manure or lime.

The amount of space given to each group of vegetables is unlikely to be the same, so the rotation cannot be rigidly followed. However, it is important to stick to it as far as possible, because it does help to limit the spread of disease and allows for a sensible programme of manuring and liming. **17**

SALAD PLANTS

Lettuce

The main types of lettuce are –
Butterhead (heads of soft, tender leaves): All the Year Round, spring, summer and autumn sowing; Avondefiance, summer sowing.
Crisp-hearted (large, crisp hearts): Webbs Wonderful; Avoncrisp.
Cos (elongated, crisp heads): Little Gem, early dwarf; Lobjoit's Green, large.
Non-hearting (pick and come again leaves): Salad Bowl.

GROWING LETTUCE
The soil should be rich in humus and able to hold moisture in summer.

Sowing and transplanting. For early summer crops sow in peat blocks under glass towards the end of winter, two seeds to a block. After hardening off, plant out under cloches in early spring.

In spring and summer sow outdoors in drills ½in (1cm) deep, and thin by stages – dwarfs and non-hearting types to 6in (15cm), butterheads and large cos, 10in (25cm), crisp-hearted types 12in (30cm) apart. To avoid gluts sow little and often – each week or so in warm weather – but at longer intervals in earlier, cooler months. Lettuce germinates badly in hot weather.

Harvesting. Depending on varieties and the time of the year when seed is sown, butterhead, crisphead and cos lettuce will be ready to harvest two to three months after sowing. Pull the lettuce out with the roots, which should not be left lying about.

Leaf Lettuce

Lettuce leaves without hearts can be grown in two ways. Choose Salad Bowl varieties and sow in April and May as with other lettuce. Thin to 6in (15cm) apart. The lettuce are not pulled up; the leaves are picked as needed and new ones grow.

Seed of cos varieties can also be used to provide leaf lettuce if they are grown so close together that they do not heart. Choose **19**

Lobjoit's Cos or Valmaine. Sow in rows 5in (13cm) apart and about 12-14 seeds to each foot (30cm). At that spacing no thinning is done. Leaves should start to be ready for picking six weeks later. The stumps are left in the ground and produce a further crop of leaves. This is a very economical use of ground.

Chicory

There are several forcing varieties, such as Witloof, which provide the chicons for winter salads, and non-forcing, notably Pain de Sucre (Sugar Loaf), rather like a cos lettuce, for late autumn.

GROWING CHICORY

Choose a part of the garden well manured for a previous crop.

Sow Witloof seed from early to mid-June, in ½in (1cm) drills, 12in (30cm) apart. Thin seedlings to 10in (25cm). Sow Pain de Sucre seed June-July. Thin to 15in (38cm). Hoe to kill weeds; water in dry weather.

Harvesting. October-November. Dig up a few roots for forcing. Cut off the tops just above the crown. Plant the roots close together in a box of soil or sand and cover the box with a lid to exclude all light. Alternatively, plant them in a pot and cover with another pot with the drainage hole plugged to block out all light. Keep at not less than 50°F (10°C). In a month or so the chicons will be about 6in (15cm) long and ready to eat. In November, when the leaves have died back, lift the rest of the crop and keep in a cold, frostproof room. Force some at intervals of three to four weeks. Pick at the very last moment before you need them, or they will go limp.

The heads of the non-forcing chicories will be ready for cutting in late autumn for immediate use. If they are to be cut later, they will need to be protected under cloches. **21**

Endive

Another alternative to lettuce. Moss Curled is for use in late summer; Batavian Broad-leaved, which looks more like a lettuce, is for autumn and winter cropping.

GROWING ENDIVE

A rich soil is needed in a slightly shaded part of the garden, so that the endive does not run to seed in summer. Sow the curled varieties in late June, where they are to grow, in drills ½in (1cm) deep. Thin to 12in (30cm). Make a further sowing three weeks later. Sow Batavian endive in August. Put late-sown plants under cloches for use until the end of the year.

Harvesting. Endive must be blanched or it will be bitter. Three or four months after sowing, cover plants with large flower pots with the holes blocked. (Do not cover plants when they are wet or they will rot.) In about three weeks the leaves will be creamy coloured and crisp. To blanch Batavian endive, tie the leaves together tightly to exclude light from the heart.

Corn Salad

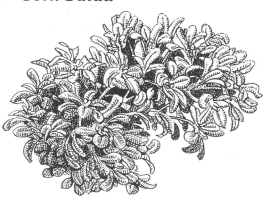

A hardy plant which tastes similar to lettuce. Sow corn salad in a sunny, humus-rich part of the garden. Fork the soil lightly and rake it to a fine tilth. Sow the seeds in mid-August and mid-September in drills 1in (2.5cm) deep and 10in (25cm) apart. Use cloches to cover the plants in winter. Pick a leaf or two from mature plants when needed.

Watercress

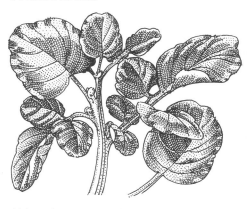

Although watercress is an aquatic plant, it can be grown without running water in a dank and shady part of the garden.

23

Dig a trench 24in (60cm) wide and 12in (30cm) deep. At the bottom put 6in (15cm) of well-decayed manure or compost. Cover with 3in (8cm) of soil. Make it firm and water it well. In early summer buy a bunch or two of healthy looking watercress and plant those cuttings which have some roots on them. Set them 4in (10cm) apart each way. Water them assiduously. As they grow, pinch out the growing tips to make them bushy. Cut them right back if they start to flower.

Watercress can also be raised from seed sown in spring.

Mustard and Cress

A fast-growing salad which, indoors or out, can be harvested the year round.

In winter sow indoors. Fill a seed tray with moist soil or peat compost. Scatter the cress seeds and press them down with your hand. Cover the tray with paper until the seeds germinate. Since mustard germinates faster than cress, sow it four days later, either over the cress or in a separate box. Sow about every fortnight and cut with scissors 15-20 days later.

24   From spring to September sow outdoors.

American Cress

Similar in flavour, but easier to grow than watercress, American cress also needs shade and considerable dampness.

GROWING AMERICAN CRESS

Sow the seeds thinly every three weeks from April to August in ½in (1cm) drills, 10in (25cm) apart. Germination takes up to three weeks. Thin to 6in (15cm) apart. Cut the cress eight to ten weeks after sowing while the shoots are still young and tender. To prolong the crop into winter, cover the late-sown rows with cloches.

Pests and diseases of salad plants.

Millipedes, which are slow-moving vegetarians, attack the roots of young lettuce. To catch them, punch holes in the bottom and sides of tin or plastic containers and fit them with wire or string handles. Fill the containers with potato peelings and bury them upright alongside the lettuce. Lift and empty the containers regularly and destroy the contents.

Slugs are also a menace. Use slug baits to kill them.

The fungus botrytis causes grey mould on stems and leaves. Spray with a fungicide.

25

BRASSICAS

Preparing the soil

In the normal three-year rotation of crops
(see page 17), brassicas are planted where
peas and beans grew the previous year,
when the bed would have been well manured. If the cabbage patch was not manured
for the previous crop, manure or compost
will have to be provided.

Brussels sprouts need more feeding than
cabbages and cauliflowers are positively
greedy. At the same time they must not be
given too much nitrogen, which makes them
flabby and less able to survive winter.

Brassicas, especially Brussels sprouts and
cauliflowers, need a firm soil, so the plot
should be dug months in advance, to give
the soil time to settle.

Lime is also important. An acid soil
encourages club root – the scourge of
brassicas.

Seedbeds for brassicas

Brassicas are usually raised in seedbeds and
transplanted. A highly fertile soil is needed.
After levelling and raking it, cover the bed
with mature sifted compost. Rake it lightly.
Make shallow drills with a stick, 6in (15cm)
apart, and sow the seeds thinly. Cover them
with a scattering of compost and firm the
surface with the head of a rake. Water the
bed well the day before transplanting the
seedlings.

Cabbage

It is possible to eat cabbage all the year
round. Whether or not you wish to do so will
depend on how much of the garden you can
spare for a space-consuming crop and how
well the end product is cooked (overcooking
cabbage is a common culinary crime).

Varieties to cover most of the year include –
Spring cabbage: Durham Early; Harbinger;
Offenham Flower of Spring; April.
Summer and autumn cabbage: Hispi F_1;
Marner Allfruh; Minicole; Winnigstadt.
Winter cabbage: Jupiter F_1; Celtic F_1.
Savoy cabbage: January King.

Offenham Flower of Spring

GROWING CABBAGE

For the preparation of beds for sowing and
growing brassicas, see page 26.

Spring cabbage: sow thinly in drills ½in
(1cm) deep at the end of July in cold areas
and in August in warm areas. The seed can
be sown where the plants are to grow in rows
14in (36cm) apart. Thin first to prevent
overcrowding and later to about 4in (10cm)
apart in the row if they are to be used as
spring greens, but 12in (30cm) apart if they
are to be grown on to heart. Alternatively
they can be raised in a seedbed and transplanted at similar spacings in September.
Ready for harvesting around March to May.

CABBAGE

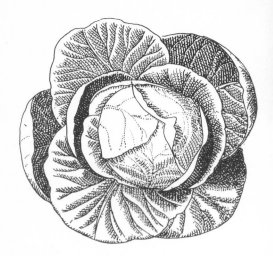

For cutting in summer: Minicole

For cutting in summer: Hispi F₁

Summer cabbage: sow the seed in early March under cloches, or in late March/early April outdoors. Thin the seedlings to 1in (2.5cm) apart when large enough to handle.

They are ready to leave the seedbed in May or early June when the plants are about 4in (10cm) high. Plant them 18in (45cm) apart in rows also 18in (45cm) apart. Hoe carefully as cabbages hate disturbance. Never let them get dry. Harvesting will be through August and September.

Winter cabbage: after watering the seedbed sow the seeds outdoors in shallow drills in late April or early May. In July plant out the seedlings 18in (45cm) apart, in rows also 18in (45cm) or a little more apart. They will be ready for harvesting from late October to November.

For cutting in winter: January King (Savoy)

Savoy cabbage: sow in late April or early May and plant out in July. They will be ready for cutting through the early winter.

29

Chinese Cabbage

Cabbage with a delicate flavour, eaten either raw or lightly cooked, especially stir-fried, to keep its crispness. Try Pe-Tsai, Sampan (F_1) or Tip Top (F_1).

GROWING CHINESE CABBAGE

Needs fertile soil in a slight shade. Sow July onwards, a little and often because it grows quickly and is liable to bolt. The large seeds are spaced 4in (10cm) apart in ½in (1cm) drills, with 12-18in (30-45cm) between rows. Thin to 8in (20cm) apart. When they begin hearting, tie the leaves together with raffia.

Harvesting. They will be ready for cutting about nine weeks after sowing.

Red Cabbage

Needs a long growing season. Red Drumhead is the favourite variety.

GROWING RED CABBAGE

Sow in August or early September in a seedbed in shallow drills 6in (15cm) apart. Thin the seedlings in the bed if over-crowded. Plant them out in April when they are about 4in (10cm) high, spacing them 24in (60cm) apart each way. They will be ready for harvesting in autumn.

Brussels Sprouts

Brussels sprouts are one of the great vegetables of autumn and winter – but only if they are properly grown (solid buttons) picked at the right moment (when small), and correctly cooked (not overcooked).

Many of the older varieties have been superseded by F_1 hybrids, which carry many small sprouts crowded on the stem. Among the ever-growing number of these hybrids are Peer Gynt (for picking October to December), and Citadel (December to March). The snag about the F_1 hybrids is that their sprouts tend to mature at the same time unlike the non-hybrid varieties which, although less prolific, produce their sprouts over a longer period. Among non-hybrids, Roodnerf varieties would be a good choice.

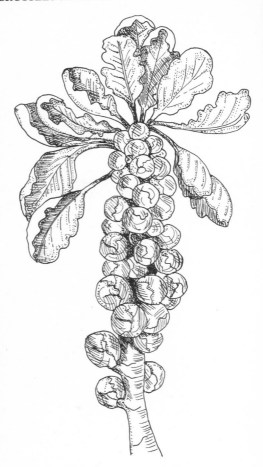

GROWING BRUSSELS SPROUTS
Brussels sprouts need a fertile soil, preferably manured for a previous crop. Dig the
bed in the autumn to give the soil time to
settle. This is vitally important, for a loose
soil produces blowsy sprouts. Lime in winter if necessary.

Seed can be sown in February in a frame
or outdoors from mid-March to April in a
seedbed. Sow thinly in drills ½in (1cm)
32   deep and 10in (25cm) apart. To prevent

Solid buttoned (left); blowsy ones (right)

overcrowding, thin the seedlings to 3in (8cm) apart.

Plant out from May as soon as the weather allows; sprouts need a long growing season. Choose a fairly damp day and plant out in the cool of the evening to help the seedlings to make a quick recovery. The spacing depends on the size and vigour of the variety, but allow 24-36in (60-90cm). Do not skimp on space; you will discover why when you pick the sprouts on cold, wet winter days. When planting, firm the soil round each plant.

In summer water and hoe if necessary. In autumn take off any yellowing leaves on the plants and draw a little soil round the stem of each plant to give support against the wind.

Harvesting. September to March. Pick the sprouts when they are big enough (i.e., not too small), working from the bottom of the stem. They can (lazily) be snapped off, but cutting with a sharp knife causes less damage.

33

CAULIFLOWERS

Cauliflowers

Cauliflowers are an immensely popular vegetable – hence the effort made to have them on sale all the year round. But to grow them in the garden all the year round is a different matter; only gardeners living in a mild climate and owning a greenhouse to start off the seeds in mid-winter can hope for that. The easier alternative is to adopt the new system of close planting, to produce mini-cauliflowers which can be frozen for the bleak periods of the year. Gardeners labouring in a really cold climate can gamble on having an unusually mild winter or, better still, growing sprouting broccoli instead. For a fairly continuous supply of fresh curds for much of the year, choose from the following varieties:

Summer cauliflowers: Alpha, Mechelse Classic, Dominant, maturing mid-June to mid-July if sown in heat in the middle of January and planted out in March; Dok Elgon, ready mid-July to mid-August if sown in a frame in March and planted out in mid- to late May, or ready in late August to September if sown outdoors in late April and planted out in June.

Autumn cauliflowers: Flora Blanca (large) or the more compact Australian varieties, Barrier Reef, ready late October, and Canberra, ready in November, when sown outdoors from mid-April to mid-May and planted out in late June.

Winter cauliflowers (more properly described as heading broccoli): most will survive only in the mildest coastal areas, so the best general choice is among the several strains of Walcheren Winter, for harvesting from March to late April or May, when sown outdoors in late May and transplanted in late July.

34

GROWING CAULIFLOWERS

Cauliflowers, like Brussels sprouts, need to grow in a firm soil, so dig the bed well in advance of planting. Choose a fairly sunny site; for winter varieties, it should also be sheltered.

The first sowings of the summer varieties are made in gentle heat, 55°F (13°C), in a greenhouse in January. Cauliflowers are fussy about being transplanted and are liable to produce small buttons instead of proper heads. Sowing in peat pots is therefore desirable. Harden off in readiness for planting out in April.

If sowing outdoors in a seedbed, wait until early April and sow thinly in shallow drills, 6in (15cm) apart. Cover the seeds with a sifting of compost. Firm the surface with a rake. If the weather is dry, keep the seed bed moist, using a fine rose. Thin the seedlings

For cutting in autumn: Canberra

to 3in (8cm) apart. Transplant in June, 24in (60cm) apart each way, planting them no deeper than they were in the seedbed. Bend some of the leaves over the developing curd to prevent it from being yellowed by the sun. Autumn varieties are raised outdoors in the same way, sowing from mid-April and transplanting in late June. In late summer it is a sensible precaution to draw soil round the stems of the cauliflowers for support – they resent being rocked in the wind.

For cutting in early spring: Walcheren Winter

Winter varieties – the heading broccoli – are sown in late May and transplanted in late July, 24-30in (60-75cm) apart each way. For protection against frost and snow, bend a few leaves over the curd.

GROWING MINI-CAULIFLOWERS

Very close planting will produce curds no bigger than 3in (8cm) in diameter, enough for a single helping and very convenient for freezing whole. Alpha, Snowball, and Garant are suitable varieties. They are grown in blocks, not in rows, and close together to keep them small. It is better to sow where the plants are to grow, rather than transplant them, causing setbacks. Sow in drills 9in (23cm) apart and thin to 4in (10cm) apart in the row. They tend to mature at the same time; this is fine if they are wanted only for freezing, but if you want a steady supply over a longer period for eating fresh, make small successional sowings from April onwards.

Broccoli

Besides the heading broccoli known as winter cauliflowers, there are white and purple sprouting broccoli and green sprouting or calabrese (the increasingly popular spears, usually encountered frozen).

Early Purple Sprouting is ready in February and March, and Late Purple Sprouting in April. Early White Sprouting is harvested in March/April and Late White Sprouting in April/May.

GROWING BROCCOLI
Sow thinly in April in a seedbed. Thin the seedlings if they are overcrowded. Transplant May/June when the young plants are 4in (10cm) high. Leave 24in (60cm) between plants and 30in (75cm) between rows. Plant firmly.

Harvesting. February to May. Cut the centre head first and thereafter keep cutting the side shoots when still young, or they will run to seed and exhaust the plant. Constant cutting produces more shoots until the plant seeds, in May or June.

Calabrese

Calabrese is not as hardy as sprouting broccoli but, in compensation, it has a much more delicate flavour. It first grows a main cauliflower-like head; when that has been cut, side shoots appear. These taste even better than the first head. There are two popular F_1 hybrids: Express Corona, which produces many spears, and Green Comet, which grows a larger head but has fewer spears. Both are early croppers.

GROWING CALABRESE

Sow in a seedbed in early April and thin the seedlings to avoid overcrowding. Transplant when 3in (8cm) high, spacing them 12in (30cm) apart in rows 24in (60cm) apart. Plant firmly.

Harvesting. July to September. Cut the centre head before it flowers. Side shoots begin to appear about two weeks later. Remove the side shoots with about 4-6in (10-15cm) of stem.

Kohlrabi

This is a cabbage with a swollen stem, which looks like a turnip growing out of the ground. Unlike turnips, kohlrabi can be grown in places where the summers are hot and dry – it withstands heat and drought. It prefers a light but fertile soil, not lacking in lime. White Vienna, Purple Vienna and Rowel F_1 are the usual varieties.

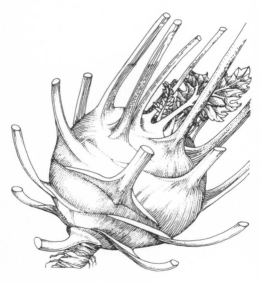

GROWING KOHLRABI

Sow every three weeks from April to July in drills 1in (2.5cm) deep, sowing three seeds together at spacings of 8in (20cm) along the row. Thin the seedlings as soon as they can be handled, leaving only the strongest. Use the red variety for late sowings if you want some for winter, but the taste is inferior.

Harvesting. Kohlrabi is pulled from June onwards, as needed, when the 'roots' are about 2in (5cm) in diameter. Late sowings can be lifted in October and stored in peat, but they shrivel considerably.

40

Kale

Kale is a cabbage without a solid heart or head, and the leaves are either flat or curly. It is healthy, health-giving and hardy beyond belief, but the flavour is too strong for many people.

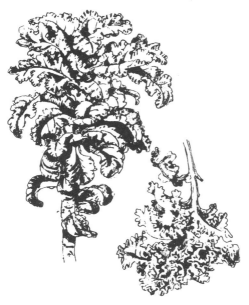

GROWING KALE

Sow the curly leaved varieties (Dwarf Green Curled or Tall Green Curled) in a seedbed in April or May. Plant out in June or July 18in (45cm) apart each way. Plant firmly. As the plants grow, firm the soil around them so that they do not blow over.

The variety Pentland Brig produces curly leaves in winter and heads like sprouting broccoli in spring.

Sow the flat-leaved varieties (Hungry Gap or Thousand-headed) in early July where they are to grow, as they do not transplant well. Thin the plants, finally to 18in (45cm) apart.

41

Brassica pests and diseases

Generally speaking, brassicas are at risk from more unpleasant pests and diseases than any other common vegetable. A complete list might deter the faint-hearted from even thinking of growing brassicas, but innumerable gardeners do escape most of the calamities, largely by giving the plants every chance to stay healthy.

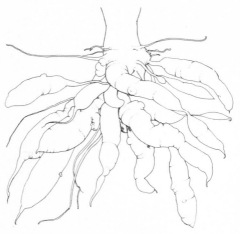

The real bogey is club root, a fungus which makes the root rot and swell and stunts growth. In a badly infected garden thousands of millions of the minute spores of the fungus can inhabit one cubic yard. Steps which can help to avoid it are:

(1) Do not grow brassicas on the same ground more than one year in three. (If the soil is already infected, avoid it altogether for at least seven years and even then the fungus may have survived.) Never grow in badly drained and acid soil. Lime well. Dig in plenty of manure or compost.

(2) Since the fungus may be introduced on the roots of seedlings bought in, make sure that they come from a reliable source and the roots show no signs of any swelling.

(3) Pull up any plant which shows evidence of disease and burn it – never leave it lying about.

(4) Keep the site as free of weeds as possible; they may be acting as hosts to pests and diseases.

(5) If you wish to take extra precautions, there are fungicides in which roots can be dipped before planting.

Not all swollen roots mean that club root has struck. The villain may be the gall weevil which burrows into the root. The swelling it causes is hollow, whereas the galls caused by club root are solid. If you cut open a gall and find a grub inside, the gall weevil is responsible. Yield is generally not greatly affected.

The caterpillars of the large and small cabbage white butterflies eat the leaves of cabbage. The yellow eggs are laid on the underside of the leaves and can be destroyed by hand or sprayed with derris.

The caterpillar of the cabbage moth burrows into the heart of the cabbage and eats it. Destroy with derris.

The small white grubs of the cabbage root fly eat the stem below soil level. Sprinkle Bromophos around the base of the young plants after transplanting.

43

SPINACH

Spinach

There are varieties grown to eat in summer, among them Norvak and Long-standing Round (it is the seeds which are round). These are less likely to bolt in hot dry weather. Among the varieties to grow for winter use is Long-standing Prickly (the seeds are prickly). Sigmaleaf can be sown in spring to eat in summer, or in autumn to eat in winter. A loamy soil is best, with slight shade for summer crops and sun for winter varieties.

GROWING SPINACH
Sow summer varieties at intervals of three weeks from March to end July in 1in (2.5cm) drills, 12in (30cm) apart. Thin to 6in (15cm) apart.

Make a sowing of a winter variety in early August and a second in September. Thin to

6in (15cm) apart. In colder areas protect with cloches from late October.

Harvesting. Summer varieties are ready to pick 8-11 weeks after sowing. Take young and tender leaves but do not strip a plant bare. Pick winter varieties sparingly, especially in bad weather.

Spinach Beet

Spinach beet, also called perpetual spinach is less temperamental than the real spinach and with a stronger flavour.

GROWING SPINACH BEET
Sow in April and July in 1in (2.5cm) drills, 18in (45cm) apart. Thin seedlings to 8in (20cm) apart when large enough to handle.

Harvesting. Keep picking the leaves to ensure a constant supply of young tender leaves, taking them from the outside of the plants. Do not strip them bare. Although the July sowing may be ready to pick in autumn, the real purpose is to provide leaves in winter and early spring.

STALKS AND SHOOTS

Asparagus

One of the most delectable vegetables of spring. Once the plants are established – which takes two to three years – they will go on cropping for up to ten years. Connover's Colossal, with thick, greenish white shoots, is the most widely available variety, but others include F_1 hybrids.

GROWING ASPARAGUS

Plants can be grown from seed, but planting one-year-old crowns gives slightly faster results. Choose a sunny part of the garden; the bed should be well drained, fertile and not lacking in lime. The success of the crop over the years depends on how well the site is prepared.

In March or April dig a trench 8in (20cm) deep and 12in (30cm) wide. If there is more than one row, put them 36-48in (90-120cm) apart. Plant the crowns 18in (45cm) apart, fanning the roots out evenly. Cover with 3in (8cm) of soil, gradually filling up the trench with the rest of the soil during the summer. When the stalks turn yellow in the autumn, cut them down near to the ground.

Each February or March give the rows 3 ounces of a general fertilizer to the square yard (90g to 1 sq metre). Then mound up the soil a few inches along the rows.

Harvesting. No spears should be cut for the first two years and in the third year only a few should be taken from each plant. The following year cutting starts around the end of April, when the shoots are about 4in (10cm) above the ground. The cuts are made below soil level; there are special knives which make this rather tough job easier. Cutting should not go on longer than six weeks. Overcropping harms the following years' yields.

Towards the tenth year the bed will deteriorate. To avoid waiting while a new bed establishes itself, add another row each year to the existing bed, after about the fourth year.

Pests and diseases

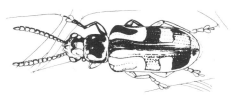

Asparagus beetles and grubs may devour, perhaps strip, foliage in summer. Spray with derris.

The most serious disease is the fungus which causes violet root rot; the foliage turns yellow and dies. The fungus spreads throughout the bed. Start a new bed elsewhere and do not grow root vegetables on the old site for a few years.

Globe Artichoke

This edible thistle has always been considered an epicurean vegetable, but in warm, sunny areas and lightish fertile soil it is reasonably easy to grow. The parts eaten are the fleshy base of the scales and the fleshy heart or *fond*. Green Globe is the variety most generally available, but the best is probably Vert de Laon.

GROWING GLOBE ARTICHOKES

Plants can be grown from seed, but it will be 2 ½ years before you will be able to pick a globe. Instead, buy offsets – rooted suckers, some 9in (23cm) long – from garden centres in April. Plant them 2in (5cm) deep, and 36in (90cm) apart. Water well. Remove any heads in the first year. In autumn cut down the stems and cover the crowns with leaves or straw as a protection against frost.

Harvesting. Cutting of the heads begins in the year after planting, from July to September. Cut the heads while they are still young and tender and the scales tight. The terminal bud will be ready first; the lateral heads can be picked later.

The plants will deteriorate after three years. Before they do, plant a new bed in a different part of the garden, by taking your own offsets – suckers with some roots – from around the crown of the plants.

Seakale

Seakale is easy to grow, but curiously it is often overlooked. When forced it produces white shoots, sweet and nutty flavoured. Unforced, the curly green leaves can be used in salad and the stalks eaten raw.

GROWING SEAKALE

A bed of seakale, which will go on producing for four or five years, needs a well-drained soil, rich in humus. For a worthwhile supply of shoots at least 15 plants will be needed. Seakale can be raised from seed but it is better to buy root cuttings, called thongs. The tops are usually cut straight across whereas the bottoms are cut at a slant, to show which way up they should be planted. In March plant the thongs with their tops ½in (1cm) below the surface of the soil, 12in (30cm) apart, with rows 18in (45cm) apart. As the seakale grows, remove all shoots except the strongest. Also remove flower stems and the leaves when they die down in October.

Carefully dig up the roots in November. Cut the sideshoots off the roots, when about 6in (15cm) long; these will provide next year's cuttings. Remember to cut the tops level and the bottoms slanting. Store in sand in a cool place for planting out in March.

Also store the roots in sand ready for forcing. To force, plant the roots in rich loamy soil in boxes or pots, with the crowns just showing above the surface. Cover them to exclude all light and keep them at a constant 50°F (10°C). In four to five weeks the shoots will be about 6in (15cm) long and ready for cutting. Cut just before using; they are usually steamed – but avoid over-cooking.

Florence Fennel

Not easy to grow in northern climates, but it is well worth trying if you like the sweet aniseed flavour of the bulbous stem.

GROWING FLORENCE FENNEL

It needs a rich, moisture-holding soil to encourage the stem base to swell and must be grown in a sunny position. Sow April to August, a little each month for a continuous supply. Sow in ½in (1cm) drills, 18in (45cm) apart. As the plant is not large, growing to around 24in (60cm) high, thin the seedlings to only 8in (20cm). Fennel must never go short of water. When the bulb swells to about the size of a golf ball, draw a little soil around it. After two or three weeks the bulb will have blanched and grown bigger.

Harvesting. Pull up the bulbs as needed when they are the size of a tennis ball.

51

Celery

The conventional method of growing and blanching celery takes up an inordinate amount of time. There are trenches to be dug for the young plants and several earthings up are necessary to blanch the stalks – this removes the inherent bitterness. Consequently, there is much to be said for the self-blanching varieties (for example, Golden Self-blanching, Celebrity and American Green), which are also less stringy. However, their flavour is not so pronounced and they are not winter hardy, so if you want home-grown celery for the winter you will have to go to the trouble of trenching, using such varieties as Giant White and Giant Pink.

GROWING SELF-BLANCHING CELERY

Sow the seed in March or April in trays of loam seed compost. Do not cover the seeds. Keep at a temperature of 50-65°F (10-18°C). Germination will take place in two to three weeks. Prick out into trays of loam potting compost, 2in (5cm) apart. Harden off gradually and plant out in May.

Self-blanching celery is grown closely in square blocks so that the plants blanch one another. They should be not more than 11in (28cm) apart each way and not less than 6in (15cm). This minimum spacing will produce a greater number of sticks but they will be more slender.

Keep well watered all through the summer if the weather is dry. The plants on the exposed sides of the block will not be fully self-blanching. This is remedied by wrapping a strip of black polythene round the edges of the block.

Harvesting. Lift the celery as needed from August onwards until the frosts.

GROWING TRENCH CELERY

In spring dig a trench 12in (30cm) deep and 15in (38cm) wide for a single row of celery, or 18in (45cm) wide for a double row (trickier to earth up). Put half the soil on one side of the trench and half on the other. Fork manure or compost into the bottom of the trench and cover it with soil to within 5in (13cm) of the top. (The rest of the soil will be used in earthing up.)   53

Young plants can be bought from nurseries and this saves a lot of trouble, but you can raise your own from seed sown in heat – 60°F (16°C) – in February. Prick them out when they are large enough to handle and later gradually harden them off in a cold frame.

In June plant the celery in the previously dug trench, at spacings of 9in (23cm). Water very liberally. All through the growing period the plants should be kept extremely well watered.

Earthing up begins in August when the plants are 12in (30cm) or more high. Loosely tie black polythene round the stalks of each plant. This is to prevent the soil from getting between the stalks (an abomination to the cook). Earth up only a little this first time. Three weeks later earth up rather more. The final earthing up a further three weeks later should cover the stalks. The leaves should never be covered with soil.

Harvesting. The stalks should be sufficiently blanched nine weeks after the start of earthing up. Dig up the plants as you need them, working from the end of the row.

Pests.

Leaf miner fly attacks celery plants from May throughout the summer. The larvae do the damage, tunnelling their way through the leaf tissues. Damage can be checked by destroying all affected leaves.

54

Rhubarb

Usually used as a fruit but most often grown in the vegetable plot, rhubarb's pink slender stalks can be produced in winter by forcing, while the main crop continues until mid-summer. Timperley Early and Hawke's Champagne are favourite early varieties. Sutton is good for the main crop.

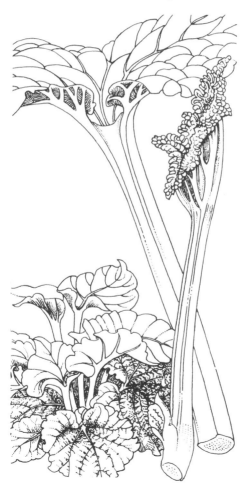

GROWING RHUBARB

The most succulent stalks are grown in fairly heavy soil, to which plenty of manure or compost has been added. Rhubarb is easy to grow from seed, but that means waiting an extra year for a crop. Sow seeds outdoors in April, 1in (2.5cm) deep, and thin to 6in (15cm). Transplant to a permanent bed in the autumn.

It is more reliable to buy roots than to raise plants from seed. Plant them when the buds are dormant, in October/November or February/March. Allow 36in (90cm) between plants and between rows. The buds should be no deeper than 2in (5cm) below the surface of the soil.

In the first year the plants will be establishing themselves so no stalks are picked. In the second year only a few may be removed and none from plants which you intend to force in the winter. After that the bed should have five years or more of useful life. Remove all flowering heads as they appear. In February give the bed a dressing of manure or compost, carefully forking it in. To keep up a supply of the three-year-old plants needed for forcing indoors, dig up a few established clumps in either October/November or February/March each year. The clumps can be divided into pieces, but each must have an undamaged bud.

Harvesting. Mid-April to July. Pull – do not cut – a stick or two from each crown as you need them, balancing your needs with what the plant is capable of producing. If you overpull you will suffer for your greed the following year with a smaller crop from weakened plants. Stop pulling in July.

Forcing rhubarb indoors. Dig up crowns, which should be at least three years old, when the leaves die back in November/December. If the roots are exposed to the cold for two weeks they will force faster. To force, lay the clumps close together in a

56

shallow box and just cover with soil. Give them a good watering. Cover with a tall box and put black polythene over it to exclude all light. Keep them indoors at 50-55°F (10-13°C). Below 45°F (7°C) growth is very slow. Above 60°F (16°C) the sticks will be spindly, pale and tasteless. Water occasionally to keep the roots moist, but not wringing wet. The sticks should be ready for pulling in five to six weeks. By staggering the times of boxing the roots, a supply can be maintained. When all the sticks have been pulled throw the roots away. They will be worn out.

Forcing rhubarb outdoors. Outdoor rhubarb can be hurried on for pulling a few weeks earlier. In mid-January or February put a bucket or box over each clump you want to force, choosing the old ones which are due to be retired. Put plenty of straw over and around the buckets or boxes to provide some warmth. (Manure, which generates more warmth, was used when there was plenty around.) This gentle forcing will provide stalks for pulling three weeks or so earlier than in the open garden.

PODS AND SEEDS

Sweet Corn

The reason for growing sweet corn – not the easiest crop – is to be able to cook and eat the cobs as soon as they have been picked; thereafter the flavour deteriorates rapidly, even within the hour, because the sugar in the kernels begins to convert to starch.

GROWING SWEET CORN

A humus-rich soil and a site in full sun, protected from wind, is necessary.

The seeds will not germinate if the soil temperature is below 50°F (10°C), so this is the regulating factor for outdoor sowings. In warm areas mid-May might be possible, especially under cloches. In drills 1in (2.5cm) deep sow two seeds together at intervals of 18in (45cm). Sweet corn is grown in blocks of short rows, to increase the chances of self-pollination. Allow 18in (45cm) between each row within the block. Keep the stronger of the two seedlings.

In colder areas sow indoors from mid-April to early May, in peat pots (to avoid root disturbance). Use loam seed compost and sow two seeds in each pot. Place in a propagator at 55°F (13°C). Discard the weaker seedling. Harden off ready to plant out in late May or early June, preferably under cloches at first. Space the plants 18in (45cm) apart.

Water in dry weather, especially when the plants are in flower. Tall plants should be given some support.

Harvesting. From the end of August. When the 'silks' (the female flowers above the tip of the cob) begin to wither, press one of the sweet corn seeds to test for ripeness. If the juice is clear you are too early; if milky, on time; if dried out, alas, too late.

59

Garden Peas

Garden peas are divided into round-seeded and wrinkled varieties. The round-seeded types are hardier and are used for early crops, but the taste is not as sweet as that of the wrinkled varieties. By including varieties that mature at different times among the first and second earlies and the maincrops, it is possible to have peas from mid-May to late autumn, provided that cloches are used to protect the earliest varieties.

GROWING GARDEN PEAS

Peas need a rich loamy soil, that has been well manured some time before sowing begins, in the autumn or early winter.

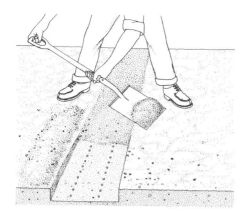

For a May-June crop sow a round-seeded dwarf variety – such as Meteor, which grows to only 12in (30cm) – under cloches during October/November. Take out a spade-wide trench, 2in (5cm) deep. In it space the seeds 2in (5cm) apart, in rows 4in (10cm) apart. Over them put the soil taken from the trench and cover with cloches.

For the main summer crops sow the sweeter, wrinkled peas from late March, perhaps starting with Early Onward followed by the very popular Onward or Hurst Green Shaft. As a rule of thumb, the rows of second early and maincrop peas should be almost as far apart as the predicted height of the plants.

For an autumn crop sow a first early variety, such as the mildew-resistant Kelvedon Wonder, in June or July.

Harvesting. From June to autumn pick the pods from the bottom of the plants as they fill. The problem with some of the newer dwarf varieties is that they produce all their pods at about the same time, ruling out a long picking period. When the crop is finished do not pull up the haulm but sever it with a hoe at soil level, leaving the roots with their nitrogen-rich nodules to benefit the soil.

Petits Pois

The aristocrat among peas and the sweetest of them all. Waverex grows to only 18in (45cm).

GROWING PETITS POIS

They need a rich soil, not short of lime. Sow from April to June for a succession of crops. Take out a shallow trench 1in (2.5cm) deep. Sow the seeds in two rows, 6in (15cm) apart each way.

Harvesting. Pick them as the pods fill. They are delicious raw.

Sugar Peas

Also known as *mangetout* because the whole pea, pod and all, is eaten. Older varieties grow inconveniently tall, but Oregon Sugar Pod and Sugar Dwarf Sweet Green are among the more manageable.

GROWING SUGAR PEAS

Sow the seeds in April in double rows in spade-wide trenches 2in (5cm) deep and 2-3in (5-8cm) apart each way. Make further sowings in May and June. Support the plants as they grow.

Harvesting. The pods will be ready for picking – before the peas swell – about two months after sowing.

Asparagus Peas

This is not a true pea, but a vetch. Nor is it related to asparagus, although it has a certain delicate, asparagus-like flavour. It is eaten whole, pod and all, but must be picked when very small or it will be tough and stringy. The brownish red flowers are most attractive.

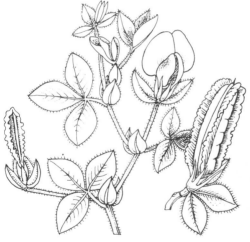

GROWING ASPARAGUS PEAS

Given a light rich soil, a sunny position and a good summer, they will crop well. They are damaged by frost. Sow under glass in April and plant out about six weeks later, 12in (30cm) apart, or sow outdoors in early May and thin to 12in (30cm). They need support.

Harvesting. Pick the pods when they are about 1in (2.5cm) long and do not overcook.

French Beans

In both cooking and cultivation the most tender bean is the French bean, otherwise known as the kidney bean, string bean and *haricot vert*. It is valuable, too, for its vitamin and mineral content. Among the flat-podded varieties are the old favourites The Prince and Masterpiece. The round pods include Tendergreen, Loch Ness (which can stand a certain amount of cold), and the creamy yellow Kinghorn Wax.

GROWING FRENCH BEANS

Choose a sunny sheltered spot, and in autumn dig in compost or manure.

French beans need a light but rich soil which must also be warm. So they cannot generally be grown without protection until mid-April or early May. However, in reasonably warm areas a start can be made in early March by putting cloches over the site where the beans are to be sown to warm up the soil. Sow the beans 2in (5cm) deep and

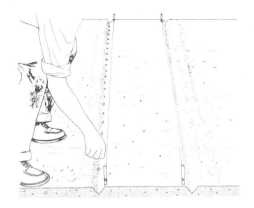

4in (10cm) apart; allow 18in (45cm) between rows. Remove the cloches during May, weather permitting.

When it is warm enough for sowing without cloches, start by raking the bed to a fine tilth a few days beforehand. At the end of the rows sow a few extra beans to fill any gaps where the beans fail to germinate. A second sowing can follow three weeks later. Another in late June will give a crop in September and October, but cloches may then be needed.

Harvesting. July/September. Pick the beans when they are about 4in (10cm) long and at their best – tender, stringless and full of flavour. Picking them young also induces the plant to go on producing more.

Runner Beans

These have a more pronounced flavour than French beans and are more widely grown. They are also prolific, which can be a drawback, for at their peak period it is almost impossible for a small family to eat them as fast as they grow. The consequence is that the pods are left on the plant too long and grow into tough, stringy monsters.

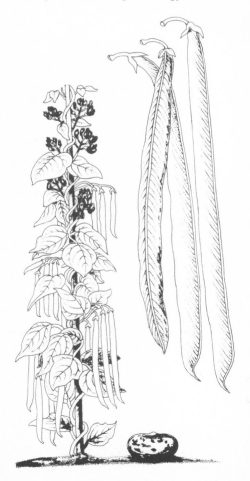

Also, as soon as beans have been allowed to mature, the plant stops producing flowers; end of crop. To prevent this, pick the pods when young, and either freeze them or throw them on the compost heap if you have a surfeit, rather than risk losing the later pods.

Two inescapable chores are staking (many varieties reach a height of 96in/240cm or more) and frequent watering, especially during flowering and as the pods start to grow.

GROWING RUNNER BEANS

Runner beans need a rich, deeply dug soil in a part of the garden not exposed to winds. In February or March take out a trench 18in (45cm) wide, to the depth of a spade, in readiness for sowing. Dig plenty of compost or well-rotted manure into the soil at the bottom of the trench.

Sow outdoors at the end of May in warm areas and in early June in colder regions – runner beans are easily damaged by frost. Allow 10in (25cm) between seeds sown in a double row, 18in (45cm) apart.

In warm areas a second sowing can be made in June for cropping in October.

The tall varieties to grow for these outdoor sowings include Achievement, Prizewinner and Streamline. There are a few dwarf varieties, notably Hammond's Dwarf Scarlet. It is often grown under cloches, sown in late April or early May, 6in (15cm) apart each way. The dwarfs do not crop as heavily as the climbers.

Put in the stakes to support the tall varieties when two leaves have opened out. The simplest way is to make an inverted 'V' frame of canes along the double row of beans, one for each plant, and reinforced by canes tied horizontally along the top.

Harvesting. Pick regularly from August to October when the beans are young and tender.

Broad Beans

Broad beans are hardier than French or runner beans, but like them they are at their best when young and very tender. A succes-

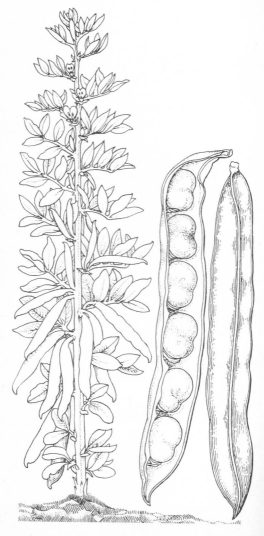

sion can be obtained by sowing Aquadulce in autumn (in milder areas), followed by Longpods under cloches in January to March and the better-tasting Windsor varieties in the open garden at intervals between March and May. Alternatively, sow only the dwarf variety, The Sutton, under cloches in autumn and without protection from late March to July.

GROWING BROAD BEANS

A well dug, well manured, fairly heavy soil suits broad beans. But November-sown crops survive the winter better in lighter soils (and sheltered gardens).

Sow broad beans in double rows, 8-10in (20-25cm) apart and 2in (5cm) deep. The easiest way is to make a hole with a trowel for each bean. If there is more than one row, allow at least 24in (60cm) between rows.

Tall varieties will have to be supported. Stick poles into the soil at intervals along both sides of each row, close to the plants. Tie twine to the poles about 12in (30cm) above ground level, so that the beans have something to lean against. When the plants have reached 24in (60cm) tie more twine further up the poles.

Beans under cloches can be decloched in early April, when they are likely to have reached the top of the cloches. (The Sutton may be small enough to stay under cloches until cropping time.) Never let the soil dry out. When flowers are setting well, pinch out the growing points, along with 6in (15cm) of stem. This helps to thwart black fly, the curse of broad beans.

Harvesting. June to September. Pick the beans when young, long before the skin of the bean has become thick and indigestible. Early picking also encourages the growth of more beans. When the crop is over, either cut the tops right down and dig the roots into the soil, or pull the plants up and put them on the compost heap. **69**

Pea pests and diseases

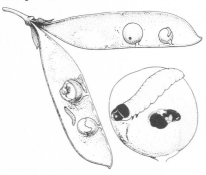

In June and July, pea moths lay the eggs which produce those familiar maggots inside the pods. No spray can reach them there at that stage, so the pest has to be tackled earlier by spraying with an insecticide a week or so after flowering starts. Alternatively, you can take action in the winter to lessen the menace the following year. The pupae hibernate not far below the surface. If the ground is dug shallowly in winter, birds will help to dispose of the chrysalids.

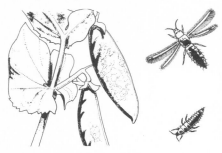

Thrips, small black insects, suck sap from the leaves and pods, discolouring and distorting them and reducing the yield. Spray with derris at the picking stage.

White powdery patches on leaves are mildew. Watering in August/September helps to prevent it; spraying with Bordeaux mixture helps to control it.

70

Bean pests and diseases

Blackfly is the aphid which adores broad beans. Spray with derris or pyrethrum. The fly attacks young juicy shoots; remove the temptation by pinching out 6in (15cm) of the stem tips when plenty of pods have formed.

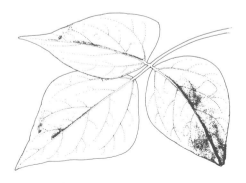

Halo blight is indicated by semi-transparent spots, surrounded by a yellow ring, on the leaves and pods of French beans. Spray with a weak Bordeaux mixture. 71

THE ONION FAMILY

Onions

Onions can be grown from seed or from sets, which are small bulbs raised from seed the previous year (usually by specialist growers). Although sets are more expensive, they are likely to produce a more dependable crop in areas where the climate (eg. short and wet summers) is less than ideal for growing from seed. Varieties grown as sets include Stuttgart Giant and Sturon.

GROWING ONIONS FROM SETS

Buy small bulbs, around ½in (1cm) in diameter; larger bulbs are likely to bolt (flower prematurely) unless they have been heat treated, as many sets are. Plant them in a firm bed in late March or April – not before. If planted 2in (5cm) apart, in rows 10in (25cm) apart, there will be a good crop of medium-sized onions. If planted 4in (10cm) apart the onions will be larger, but there will be fewer of them.

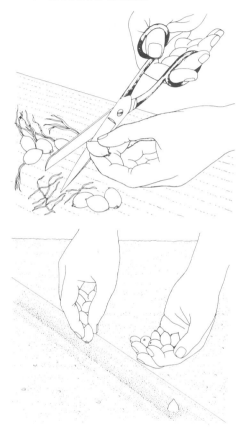

Before planting snip off the dead tips of the bulbs, so that birds cannot get much of a grip to pull them out of the ground. They should be planted deep enough for the tips to show just above the soil.

Harvesting. The onions can be lifted in August. Dry them outdoors if there is any sun, but indoors if they are likely to get wet.

GROWING ONIONS FROM SEED

Choose a sunny part of the garden where the soil is fertile and dig the bed well in advance so that it has time to settle firmly.

Seed of some varieties can be sown in autumn outdoors and overwintered, but losses are often heavy. Seed can also be sown in a heated greenhouse or propagator in January, but outdoors the time for spring-sown varieties is March and April. There are several excellent Rijnsburger varieties (globe shaped). Bedfordshire Champion, (large globe) and Giant Zittau (semi-flat bulbs) are old favourites, and there is an increasing number of F_1 hybrids.

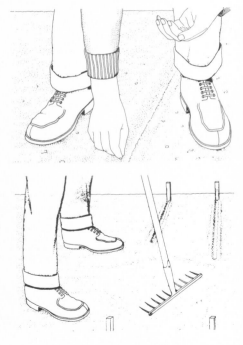

Sow the seeds thinly in shallow drills, 12in (30cm) apart, and barely cover them with fine soil or sifted compost. Firm the rows with the back of a rake.

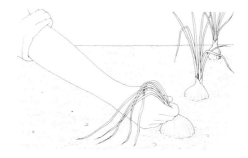

Thin first to 2in (5cm) and then to 3in (8cm). Do not leave thinnings lying about as they will attract onion fly. Weed the rows by hand so that the bulbs are not damaged by hoeing. Water in dry weather, but stop as soon as the bulbs begin to ripen, from late July to August. In a dry summer the leaves will topple over on their own. In a wet summer they may have to be bent over to encourage them to dry off. In a very wet summer the onion may go on growing leaves, producing bull-necked onions which will not ripen.

Harvesting. In August/September, when the leaves have turned yellow and shrivelled, the onions will be ready to harvest. Choose a dry day. If the bulbs are ripe they can be pulled up by hand or eased with a fork. If the weather is thoroughly settled, spread the onions on sacking or on a raised wire-netting frame (see page 76). In uncertain weather spread the bulbs out indoors or in a well-ventilated frame; they must not get wet. Only when the skins are brittle is it safe to store the onions in a dry, cool, frostproof place. The Dutch trays used by greengrocers are one possibility. Fill the trays with one layer of onions and stack them on top of each other.

Alternatively, onions can be successfully stored by stringing them, a method which takes up less room (see the illustration on page 77).

Drying and storing onions

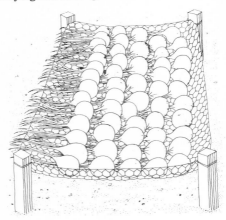

Getting onions dry enough to store can be a problem. In the absence of sun, good circulation of air is necessary. A raised wire-netting frame helps to achieve this. Use it outdoors in dry weather or indoors in an airy shed.

To string onions for storing, take a length of stout string or twine and tie it to form a loop. Hang the loop over a hook at a convenient height and proceed by the following stages. The first attempts may produce straggly results, but with practice a professional look develops.

76

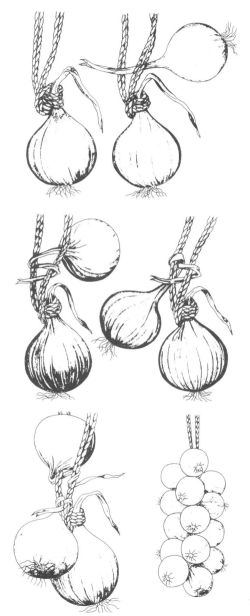

Shallots

These are small, mild onions. They are planted as small bulbs which produce clusters of identical bulbs – anything from six to a dozen. Varieties are Dutch (or Long Keeping) Yellow, and Dutch (or Giant) Red; both store well for eight months or more. Hative de Niort, the expensive three-star variety, looks attractive but does not keep as well.

GROWING SHALLOTS

Grow in a bed prepared and manured the previous autumn to give it time to settle firmly. Plant as early as possible, in February/March, having trimmed off any long, dead leaves. Space them 6in (15cm) apart, with 9-12in (23-30cm) between rows. Leave the top of each bulb above ground. In June draw the soil slightly away from the clusters of bulbs to ripen them.

Harvesting. In June/July, when the leaves have turned yellow, dig up the shallots. Leave them in the sun to dry until the skins are brittle. Keep some bulbs to plant the following year. Store the rest in a cool place in string bags for use in winter. Remove any going bad.

Chives

Chives are grown for their delicately flavoured leaves.

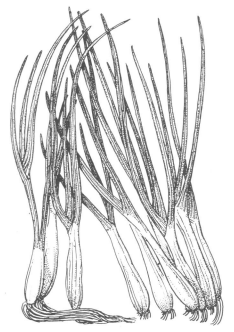

GROWING CHIVES
They can be raised from April-sown seed, but for quicker results buy clumps of bulbs in spring. Plant about six bulbs together at 8in (20cm) intervals in a row. Constant cutting is essential to keep up a fresh supply of leaves. Every three years lift the clumps, divide them and plant them in another part of the garden. Although perennial, they are not evergreen, so if you want chives in winter dig up a clump in autumn, replant in a pot and place on an indoor windowsill.

Salad Onions

Larger and more strongly flavoured than chives, salad (or spring) onions are eaten raw. White Lisbon is the old favourite, but the newer Ishikura variety produces long white stems without bulbing.

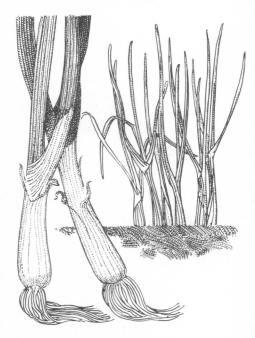

GROWING SALAD ONIONS

Choose a part of the garden which has been manured for a previous crop. For the earliest spring crop sow, fairly thickly, under cloches in August or early September in ½in (1cm) drills, 10in (25cm) apart. For cropping from June onwards, sow under cloches in February or in the open in March/April. Sow again in May/June for use in autumn. Weed carefully by hand throughout.

Harvesting. Pull the onions when they are big enough to use.

Garlic

The most strongly flavoured of the onion tribe, garlic is grown from the cloves which form the bulb.

GROWING GARLIC

Garlic does best in a well-manured light soil and in sun. Remove the papery skin from a bulb and separate it into cloves. Plant the cloves from January to March, but the earlier the better, 4in (10cm) apart and about 1in (2.5cm) deep. The tip of the clove should be level with the surface of the soil. Weed well, by hand to avoid hoe damage.

Harvesting. When the stems and leaves lose their greenness and topple over, take up the bulbs, easing them out of the ground with a fork. Dry them outside in the sun if possible, but indoors if the weather is uncertain. After drying, hang them up in a string bag. Save as many as you need of the sturdy outside cloves for planting your next crop.

Leeks

Leaving aside any obsessive desire to raise mammoth, cup-winning specimens, leeks are much easier to grow than onions. They also have the virtue of being hardy. Lyon is a favourite variety for autumn use. Musselburgh is good for harvesting from January to April.

GROWING LEEKS
Although leeks are not as greedy as onions, no harm is done by giving them the same treatment. In the previous autumn, dig in plenty of compost or rotted manure where the leeks are to grow. Sow outdoors in a

seedbed in March/April, depending on the weather, in drills 1in (2.5cm) deep.

Mid- to late June is the time to transplant the seedlings, when they are 6-8in (15-20cm) tall. Lightly fork over and then rake the soil where the leeks are to go. Using a garden line to get a straight row, make holes with a large dibber 6in (15cm) deep. Leeks planted 9in (23cm) apart will give an optimum crop of average-sized leeks; closer planting produces a greater number of more slender leeks. Lift the seedlings carefully from the seedbed. A handfork is least likely to damage them. Lower a leek into each hole, then gently pour a little water into the hole. That is all that is needed; do not firm the soil.

If there is more than one row, leave 12in (30cm) between them. This allows room to draw up the soil round the growing plants at intervals, producing longer, whiter leeks.

Harvesting. November/April. Lift the leeks with a fork, as needed.

Onion pests and diseases

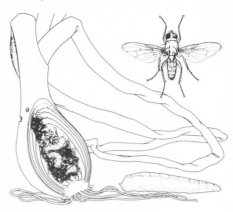

The onion fly is the curse of the onion family, although onion sets, shallots and leeks are less vulnerable than onions themselves. It lays its eggs in the soil; the maggots which emerge burrow into the bulbs and eat them. The leaves yellow and die. The smell of thinnings attracts the fly so they should never be left lying about. Dust round the seedlings with calomel dust.

84 Eelworms are like transparent eels, but they are so small that they cannot be seen by the naked eye. They burrow into the bulbs and then into the stems which go soft and swell. They have a phenomenal rate of reproduction – an infected bulb could contain millions of them. Burn all affected plants and do not grow onions on the same ground for at least five years after an outbreak. Chickweed is a host to this eelworm, hence the importance of keeping a weed-free onion bed.

Onion smut is easily recognizable: the diseased young onion leaves are covered with blisters, which contain black, powdery spores. To avoid onion smut, water the drills before sowing with a solution of ¼ pint of formalin in four gallons (125ml in 18 litres) of water.

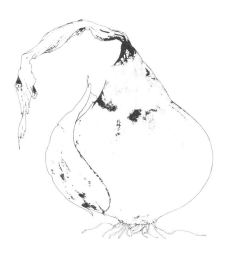

Neck rot and bulb rot are caused by one of the botrytis fungi, producing masses of white and grey mould or brown rot on onions in store. The fungus is most likely to develop if the onions have been damaged, or have not been dried properly after harvesting, or have been stored in a damp, ill-ventilated place. Do not try to store onions with green, fleshy necks.   85

ROOTS

Carrots

Carrots are worth growing only if you have the right kind of soil. Ideally it should be light and fertile, and it must also be deep if long-rooted varieties are to succeed. In heavy and stony soil the only hope is to be satisfied with the short-rooted varieties. Heavier soil should be dug before the winter so that the frost can make it friable. Whatever the type of soil, never manure it for a crop of carrots.

Among early short-rooted varieties are Amsterdam Forcing and Early Nantes, which are sown under cloches in January to late February and pulled between mid-May and July. Medium-rooted carrots include varieties of Chanteney Red Cored, sown outdoors in April for use from August until November. Autumn King types, producing large carrots, can be sown in May to harvest in November and December.

A better alternative to these three main sowings is to make small sowings of these varieties every three or four weeks until the middle of July. This ensures a more constant supply of young carrots.

GROWING CARROTS

For the earliest crops put the cloches in position a few weeks before sowing to warm up the soil. In warm areas these sowings can begin in February, but should be later elsewhere. Thin to 2in (5cm) for cropping young. The smell of disturbed seedlings attracts carrot fly, so thin on a cloudy evening when there are fewer flies about. Water the rows afterwards and do not leave thinnings lying about.

When sowing the later crops in the open, allow 6in (15cm) between rows and thin the seedlings to 4in (10cm) apart if the carrots are to be allowed to grow bigger. Make every effort to sow thinly; this is difficult because carrot seeds are very small. Some varieties are available as pelleted seed and are worth the extra expense because the seed can be spaced to avoid thinning, with its consequent dangers.

Harvesting. Pull the carrots as they are needed, when young and tender.

Chanteney and Autumn King varieties withstand a certain amount of frost and can be stored in the ground if given protection. Do not remove the foliage when it dies, but in early December cover it with a good layer of straw. Put polythene sheeting on top to prevent the straw from becoming sodden. If carrots are left in the ground too long in wet weather the roots will start to split.

The carrots can also be stored indoors, which is more convenient for use. Lift the crop before the first frosts. Twist off the leaves and store the roots – not touching each other – in boxes in layers, covering each layer with sand. Keep in a cool, frostproof place.

Turnips

Turnips picked in their infancy in early summer are the most delicious. Snowball (globular and white-fleshed) and Purple-Top Milan (flat, white-fleshed with a purple top) are popular earlies. Later maincrop varieties include Golden Ball (yellow-fleshed and hardy) and Manchester Market (mild and white fleshed).

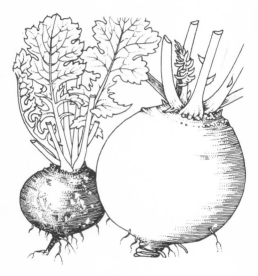

GROWING TURNIPS

Early turnips must be grown quickly. This demands a fertile, moisture-holding soil, which has been manured the year before. Sowing in the open can begin early in April, in drills ½in (1cm) deep, with rows 12-16in (30-40cm) apart. Thin first to 3in (8cm) apart when the seedlings have their first rough leaves. Two weeks later thin to 6in (15cm) apart.

Continue sowing early varieties every three weeks until the beginning of July. In late July sow seed of late varieties. Water well whenever the weather is dry; they must never go short of moisture.

Harvesting. Pull the early turnips as needed, when no smaller than a golf ball and no bigger than a tennis ball if you want them at their best.

In October the late varieties can be lifted. Twist off the tops and store the roots in boxes of sand in a cool, frostproof place.

Swedes

Larger, sweeter and hardier than turnips, they store particularly well. Marian is now the most popular variety, but Purple Top is also reliable.

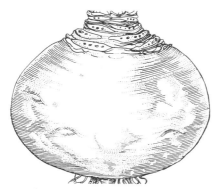

GROWING SWEDES

Swedes need a similar soil to that required for turnips. Sow in drills ½in (1cm) deep, 15in (38cm) apart. Swedes are slow growing, so in cold areas sowing begins early in May; in warm areas it is delayed until mid-June. Thin the seedlings to 12in (30cm) as soon as they are big enough to handle. Water well in dry weather.

Harvesting. Immature swedes can be pulled in late summer, and excellent they are, too. But they are mainly useful as a winter crop. They will have matured by October and can then be lifted and stored like potatoes. In mild areas, they can be left in the ground and dug up as wanted.

Beetroot

The most popular beets are now the globe (round) varieties. Most are red fleshed; for early crops there is Boltardy or Avonearly and for small late beets there is Detroit Little Ball. There is one much-liked yellow-fleshed variety, Burpee's Golden Ball, and one white-fleshed, Albina Vereduna (formerly Snowhite).

GROWING BEETROOT

Beets need a fertile soil which has not been recently manured.

For a very early crop sow Boltardy or Avonearly under cloches in early March. Follow with sowings in the open every four weeks from April until July. A sowing of the maincrop variety Detroit can be made in June or July for storing.

Beet 'seeds' are, in fact, fruits – clusters of several seeds. To help germination, soak them overnight before sowing. The seed clusters are large so they can easily be spaced in the drills, 1in (2.5cm) deep, with 8in (20cm) between rows. For the early crops put the clusters 4in (10cm) apart in the rows, but for the larger maincrop varieties space them 8in (20cm) apart. To thin, leave only the strongest seedling in the group.

Hoeing will be needed while the seedlings are young, but the fully grown beet leaves will themselves suppress most weeds. This is as well, for careless hoeing can damage the beets and make them bleed. Always keep the soil moist. If the plants are kept short of water in a warm dry spell they will tend to run to seed prematurely, and the roots will not develop properly.

Harvesting. Pull the roots for immediate use as soon as they are big enough – the smaller they are, the sweeter they will be. Twist off the leaves as soon as the beet is pulled up, leaving about 2in (5cm) of stalk. If cut they will bleed.

The main crop is lifted during a dry spell at the end of September and early October. Twist off the leaves. Store the beets, not touching each other, in boxes between layers of peat, rejecting any roots which are at all damaged; do not bruise them by careless handling. Keep in a cool, frostproof room. **91**

Parsnips

The proverbial long-rooted parsnip is no longer in great favour, except for exhibition, since it needs a great depth of soil to be grown successfully. Many varieties are also susceptible to canker, which often occurs in rich soils. The best variety to choose is probably the sweet Avonresister, most resistant to canker and only 5in (13cm) long.

GROWING PARSNIPS

The ground where the parsnips are to grow should have been manured for the previous crop. Seeds must be fresh, not left over from the previous year. Since seedlings do not transplant well, sow where the plants are to grow, as soon as the weather permits, in late February to March. Sow three of the largish seeds together, ½in (1cm) deep, at 6in (15cm) intervals in rows 12in (30cm) apart. Germination can take from two to four weeks. Thin, leaving only the strongest seedling in each group.

Harvesting. October onwards. Dig the parsnips as needed, but in November in cold areas they can be lifted and stored. In warmer areas they can be left in the ground, with only a little protection.

Celeriac

This is a celery, the base of which grows like a turnip. Marble Ball is the best known variety. It has a long growing season and needs a sunny site.

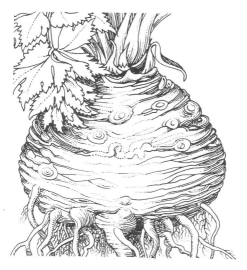

GROWING CELERIAC

The seed is sown in heat, 65°F (18°C), in March. Sow two seeds to a peat pot. Keep the strongest seedling. Harden off before planting out, at the end of May to early June. Plant 12in (30cm) apart in rows 16in (40cm) apart. The little bulbous swelling at the base of the plant must not be buried but should stay at soil level. The ground must be kept reasonably moist, although celeriac does not need such prodigious watering as celery. In September draw some soil around the swollen roots to keep them white.

Harvesting. From October dig the celeriac as needed. In November, especially in cold areas, lift the crop, remove the foliage and store the roots in peat in a cold, frostproof room. They store well.

Radishes

Summer radishes are a salad dish, munched raw. There are many varieties, from small and round to long and tapering, and from scarlet to white. Among the popular globes are Cherry Belle, which is slow to go pithy, and the quick-maturing Scarlet Globe. Saxerre is a good choice for early sowing under cloches.

The most widely grown cylindrical variety is French Breakfast, mild and crisp if pulled when young, but unpleasantly hot if left too long. If you want a white radish, which is also long (up to 12in/30cm) and tapering, try the Japanese type, Minowase Summer.

Winter radishes are often eaten cooked. They are generally stronger in flavour than the summer varieties. A mild Japanese variety (about 15in/38cm long) is Mino Early. The crisp Chinese variety China Rose is small by comparison, only 5in (13cm) long. The Spanish variety Black Spanish Round is turnip shaped and has black skin which must be peeled, and white flesh.

GROWING SUMMER RADISHES

Radishes must be grown quickly and for this they need a fertile soil – do not banish them to some spare, nondescript patch of the garden. A site manured for a previous crop is best.

The first sowings can be made under cloches in February and early March. Sow the seed thinly in the shallowest of drills, with a fine covering of soil, allowing 6in (15cm) between rows.

Outdoor sowings start in March in similar shallow drills. Always sow thinly; thick sowing produces a lot of leaves and miserably small roots. Continue the sowings every seven or ten days. Water in a hot dry spell.

Harvesting. Pull radishes when they are three to four weeks old and about ½in (1cm) across. If left in the ground longer, most varieties become hot with a texture like cotton wool.

GROWING WINTER RADISHES

Japanese varieties are sown in March for use in summer, and at the end of July to store for winter. The seeds are large enough to be spaced in twos or threes, ½in (1cm) deep and 6in (15cm) apart, in rows 12in (30cm) apart. Leave the strongest seedling of each group to grow on.

Chinese and Spanish radishes tend to run to seed if sown early, so wait until mid-July in colder areas and until late August in warmer parts, where winter sets in later. Sow in twos or threes, 8in (20cm) apart, leaving the strongest seedling to grow on.

Harvesting. Winter radishes will be ready two to three months after sowing. Late-sown varieties can be lifted at the end of October and stored in peat for the winter. The Chinese and Spanish radishes are sometimes left in the ground and dug up as needed during the winter months. But they, too, are better stored in peat.

Salsify and Scorzonera

Salsify is known as the 'vegetable oyster'; scorzonera looks like a black version of salsify, but the flesh is white and has an even better, more delicate flavour.

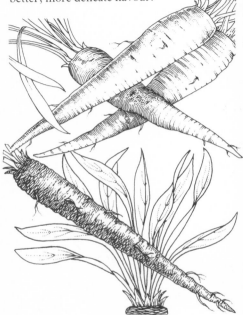

GROWING SALSIFY AND SCORZONERA

Both have long roots and need deep, fertile soil, but it must not have been recently manured. Sow in April in drills ½in (1cm) deep, in rows 12in (30cm) apart. The largish seeds can be sown in threes, 6in (15cm) apart. Thin out the weaklings. Avoid damaging the crowns when weeding.

Harvesting. In autumn lift the roots carefully (they are easily broken) as required. They are hardy enough to survive winter in the ground in most areas, but it may be convenient to lift and store them in November.

Pests and diseases of roots

Carrot fly is the most serious pest of carrots (parsnips are somewhat less vulnerable). The maggots eat the roots of the seedlings and later tunnel into the carrot itself. Seedlings emerging in late May and in August or September are most at risk. The danger of attack is reduced if care is taken when thinning; the smell of uprooted seedlings attracts the flies.

Flea beetles are a menace to turnips and swedes. They are small and black and noted for their jumping ability and voracious appetites. They eat holes in the leaves of the seedlings, possibly killing them. Dust with derris as seedlings emerge. (Flea beetles also attack brassicas, while turnips and swedes are at risk from the cabbage root fly.)

Club root is the commonest disease of turnips, as it is with cabbages (see page 42). Brown rot makes swedes hard and tasteless. The cause is boron deficiency. Water with a weak solution of borax.

TUBERS

Potatoes

There is very little point in growing most of the varieties of potatoes which can be bought in the shops. They have been bred not for taste but for profitability. Many of the older varieties which had a good flavour have disappeared because they do not crop heavily enough. Some do still exist, but tracking a supplier may prove harder than growing them.

The flavour of a potato does not, however, depend entirely on the variety; it can vary greatly with the type of soil in which it is grown – chalk, clay or loam – and the manurial treatment the soil has had. Peat can be added to heavy soil to lighten it and to lighter soil to give it body. A humus-rich soil, reinforced by digging in well-rotted manure or compost in the autumn before planting, improves the flavour, while heavy dosages of fertilizers will not. Do not lime

for this crop; potatoes prefer a slightly acid soil.

Potatoes are usually classified as first earlies (ready in June and July), second earlies (for July and August), and maincrops (for September and October, and to store for winter). Potatoes occupy a lot of room in a garden for a long period. If the garden is small it is as well to settle for an early crop, both because they are expensive to buy at that time of the year and because 'new' potatoes taste so much better when cooked straight after being dug up.

GROWING POTATOES

Encouraging the tubers, usually known as seed potatoes, to sprout before planting produces an earlier crop. Start this sprouting, called 'chitting', six weeks before the time for planting. Fibre egg boxes can be used. Place the tubers 'rose end' up – the rose end has the most eyes and is usually the widest end. Put the tubers in a cool, frostproof room, in the light, but out of the sun. This should produce sturdy shoots, ¾-1in (2-2.5cm) long, in the six weeks. Chitting is essential for the early crops and desirable for the maincrops.

POTATOES

Planting of the first earlies begins from mid-March; plan it for the time when your garden normally gets its last spring frosts. Second earlies will follow from mid-April. Take out V-shaped drills, 5in (13cm) deep, and plant the earlies 12in (30cm) apart in rows 24in (60cm) apart. Carefully cover with fine soil to avoid damaging the shoots. If the shoots of any earlies emerge during a late frost draw a little soil over them.

Maincrop planting takes place mid-April to late April. Space the tubers 15in (38cm) apart in the row, with 30in (75cm) between rows.

When the plants are about 8in (20cm) tall, use a hoe to draw the soil towards the plant from each side of the row. This earthing up will probably be enough to prevent the greening of tubers growing near the surface of the soil (caused by the sun reaching them). Indeed, potatoes can be grown successfully without earthing up. To grow on the flat, plant small seed potatoes 4in (10cm) deep, 15in (38cm) apart, in rows only 17in (43cm) apart.

Harvesting. When the flowers of the first earlies are fully open, dig up a root to see whether the potatoes are large enough to eat. If not, wait another week; but they are most desirable when small. Dig up enough for only one meal, or at most two meals. The shorter the time they are out of the ground, the easier they will be to scrape – should you wish to do so.

Later varieties for storing are left in the ground until the top growth, the haulm, has died down. Choose a dry spell for harvesting. Lever the potatoes out of the ground, working along the side of the ridges, not head-on along the rows. Pick up all tubers, however small. Any left in the ground will be a nuisance when they grow the following year and will help to perpetuate eelworms and the fungus that causes blight. Dry the potatoes on sacks in the sun. Burn all diseased tubers.

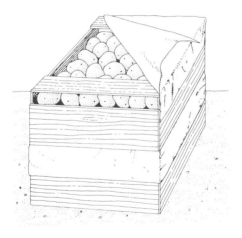

To store potatoes, spread them out on Dutch trays, stacked on top of each other and covered with black polythene to exclude all light – or they will turn green and dangerous to eat. Keep them in a cool but frostproof place; if it is too warm they will sweat and rot, but frost will also ruin them. Inspect occasionally and remove any shoots which have grown and any tubers that are going bad.

Jerusalem Artichokes

These are so easy to grow that any tubers left in the ground during harvesting will appear the following year as weeds, growing up to 10ft (3m) tall. (They are related to sunflowers.)

GROWING JERUSALEM ARTICHOKES
Plant tubers February/March, 6in (15cm) deep and 12in (30cm) apart. Staking will be necessary so that the stems do not break. cut the tops off stems in August to limit further growth.

Harvesting. The tubers will be ready for lifting from the end of October, but they taste better if they are left in the ground and dug up as needed through the winter. Save some healthy smaller tubers (1½in/3.5cm) for replanting next season.

Pests and diseases of tubers
Jerusalem artichokes are scarcely threatened by any pests or diseases, but potatoes have some serious ones to contend with.

The potato root eelworm is the major common pest. Cysts containing hundreds of eggs can stay dormant in the soil for ten

years or so. Excretions from a growing

potato activate the eggs and minute larvae burrow into the root. If they are present in overwhelming numbers the foliage dies and the crop is poor. There is no way of destroying the cysts. To prevent the build up, do not grow potatoes on the same ground two years running.

Wireworms are the yellow, tough-skinned larvae of the click beetle which bore into the tubers. They occur mainly in newly cultivated land, rather than in older gardens. To limit the damage, harvest the potatoes as soon as they are ready for lifting.

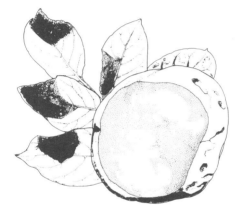

Blight, a major disease, is caused by a fungus which is carried forward from one year to the next in infected tubers. The build up starts in spring and can explode in July or August, given a few days of warm, humid weather. There is no cure. The first outward signs are dark brown marks on the leaves and stems. The haulm dies and the affected tubers rot. Burn the tubers and the haulm to lessen the risk of infection the following year. And, to repeat, never grow potatoes on the same ground two years running.

Wart disease, caused by a fungus, is less of a threat than it once was because many modern varieties are immune to it. Common scab looks nasty, but is only skin deep.

VEGETABLE FRUITS

Tomatoes

The main advance in commercial tomato breeding over the past decade has been to produce strains which crop heavily, with thick skins so that they travel well to market.

If you want to recapture the real taste of tomatoes, you will have to grow them yourself, choosing varieties for flavour rather than high yield and picking them straight off the plant. Once that would have meant owning a greenhouse, possibly heated. But here the breeders have done the

ordinary gardener proud by developing outdoor bush varieties which make tomato
growing in the open more worthwhile.
Outdoors they are still a tender crop and
they are most likely to succeed in warmer
areas, grown alongside a south-facing wall.
In colder areas the crop will be more
dependable if protected under cloches.

Bush varieties grow from 9in (23cm) to
30in (75cm) tall. They need no staking or
removal of side shoots. Most of them have
quite small fruits, but the flavour is good.
Among the best varieties are Sleaford
Abundance, Red Alert, Sigmabush F_1,
French Cross F_1, and for the earliest crops,
probably one of the subarctic varieties.

GROWING BUSH TOMATOES

During the winter dig compost and peat into
the ground where the plants are to grow.

The subarctic varieties can be sown outdoors in May and thinned to only 12in
(30cm) apart. Even in cold areas the fruits
set well and will begin to ripen in about two
months. Slightly earlier crops of these and
other varieties can be obtained by sowing
and growing under cloches. To keep the
fruits of low-growing varieties off the soil,
put polythene sheeting alongside the plants.
Cropping can go on until the first frosts.

Even earlier crops can be obtained by
using the technique of fluid sowing pre-
germinated seed (see over). This can be
used to grow tomatoes either under cloches
or in the open.

Place the cloches (or polythene tunnels) in
position towards the end of March, to warm
up the soil. Pre-germinate the seed indoors
in mid-April. Move the cloches to one side
and fluid sow to make a single row of two or
three seeds at intervals of 12in (30cm) along
the length of the cloches and at a depth of
¾in (2cm). Cover the seeds carefully and
replace the cloches straight away. The seedlings should appear in one or two weeks.
Thin as necessary. **105**

TOMATOES

Harvesting. Depending on weather and variety, cropping will extend from late August through September. Cover the plants with cloches to ripen the green tomatoes. Before the first frosts, pick any fruits that are still unripe and ripen them indoors.

How to fluid sow

In fluid sowing seed is germinated indoors, mixed with a cellulose wallpaper paste, and squeezed out along the drill in the seedbed. This method gives more even sowing in the row and because the seed is already germinated the seedlings emerge sooner.

The first step in fluid sowing is to sprout the seeds. Place several layers of paper tissues over the bottom of a plastic box. Wet the paper, and spread the seeds over it, thinly and evenly. Put the lid on and keep at a temperature of 70°F (21°C). Some seeds begin to root quickly and you must act quickly too.

Make up the wallpaper paste, which must be one without fungicide, to about half the strength for papering a wall. Gently stir the seed into the paste and pour it into an icing bag, with a nozzle ¼in (0.5cm) in diameter.

To sow take out a drill, very slightly deeper than for ordinary seed. Water it, squeeze the paste along the drill and cover with soil.

If the tomatoes are to be grown in the open, wait until the end of May before pre-germinating and sowing the seed. Space them in twos or threes, 12in (30cm) apart with 20in (50cm) between rows. Keep down weeds until the plants are large enough to smother them. Place polythene sheeting alongside the plants to keep fruits off the soil.

Cucumbers

Growing cucumbers in heated greenhouses has lost much of its attraction since the development of superior outdoor varieties of what were once the poor relations – the so-called ridge cucumbers. (They are no longer grown on ridges – they do quite well on the flat.) Good varieties include Burpless Tasty Green F_1, 8-10in (20-25cm) long; Sweet Success F_1, all female plants, growing to 12in (30cm) long and usually seedless; and the sweet, apple-shaped yellow variety, Crystal Apple.

Of course they crop later than indoor varieties for the simple reason that cucumber seed does not germinate well until the soil temperature has reached at least 55°F (13°C), and therefore cannot be sown in the open until early June. They will fruit from

early August. Sowing under cloches or in frames produces slightly earlier fruits, but to have cucumbers in May or June you will need a heated greenhouse.

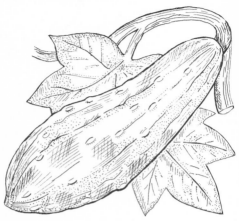

GROWING OUTDOOR CUCUMBERS

They need a humus-rich soil, well draining, in the sun and out of the wind. The easiest way to prepare the ground for the few plants which will be needed is to dig holes for them in May. They should be 12in (30cm) square, 12in (30cm) deep and 18-24in (45-60cm) away from each other. Fill with soil mixed with compost or rotted manure. Cover each position with a cloche to warm the soil. In early June plant two seeds edgeways in the centre of the pockets and put back the cloches for a few weeks. Remove the weaker seedling when the first true leaves have appeared.

Alternatively, seed can be sown indoors in a heated propagator, 65-70°F (18-21°C), at the end of April, for planting out in late May or early June. Use peat pots to avoid too much disturbance when transplanting, which cucumbers resent. Plant one seed, edgeways, in each pot. The plants must be thoroughly hardened off before they are placed out of doors.

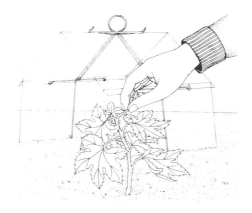

When the young plants have grown seven leaves, pinch out the growing tips to encourage the growth of side shoots. These can be allowed to trail, but they are really climbers like vines and they can be given supports to grow up. They may well crop better that way.

Do not remove male flowers. Unlike frame cucumbers, which grow bitter if they are pollinated, these outdoor varieties have to be fertilized if they are to fruit at all, but in the open it can be left to the bees.

Harvesting. From the end of July or early August onwards. If you pick them when they are small, the plants will go on producing more fruits. Ridge cucumbers are prolific if well fed, some plants producing up to 40 cucumbers. Do not wrench them from the plant; use a sharp knife.

Gherkins

Gherkins, which are raised like ridge cucumbers, are grown for pickling. Varieties include Venlo Pickling and Hokus.

They are always sown where they are to grow, in early June. Allow 24in (60cm) between plants. Pick them when they are 2-3in (5-8cm) long.

Marrows and Squashes

Marrows, squashes and pumpkins are all members of the cucumber family. Mammoth marrows are out of fashion – courgettes have ousted them.

Tender and True and Green Bush Improved are good varieties of bush marrows; Table Dainty is one of the trailers, which can be grown up fences. Summer squashes include the Custard Marrows, both white and yellow.

GROWING MARROWS AND SQUASHES

Rich soil and sun are essential. Dig holes 12in (30cm) square, 36in (90cm) apart for bush varieties and 48in (120cm) apart for trailers. Fill the holes with a mixture of soil, peat, well-rotted manure or compost. Sow seeds in peat pots, because marrows dislike root disturbance. Sow in April in a greenhouse at 65°F (18°C); at the end of April or early May in an unheated greenhouse or frame; and outdoors from mid-May, where the plants are to grow.

In early June plants raised indoors can be planted out, after hardening off.

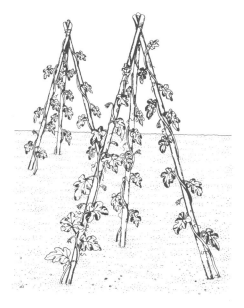

When shoots of trailers are 36in (90cm) long, pinch out growing tips to encourage fruit-bearing side shoots. If grown up tripods or against fences, pinch out at 60in (150cm). Bush varieties need no stopping.

Harvesting. July onwards. Cut the marrows while still young and the plant will go on producing more. They are easily damaged by frost, so harvest them before there is any danger of that. Hang the marrows for storing in string bags in a frostproof place.

Courgettes

Courgettes (or zucchini) are basically marrows picked when young and small, but as they have become so popular more and more varieties have been bred to produce numerous small fruits rather than a few large ones. Among them are Zucchini F_1, Aristocrat F_1, Onyx F_1, and the yellow Golden Zucchini and Golden Rush F_1.

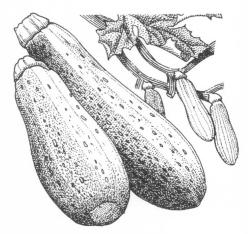

GROWING COURGETTES

Like marrows, courgettes need a rich soil and sun. They do not germinate well if soil temperature is below 55°F (13°C). For early crops, sow seed in heat, 65°F (18°C), in late April. After soaking the seeds overnight, sow two seeds 1in (2.5cm) deep, and edgeways – not flat – in each (peat) pot. Remove the weaker seedling. Harden off before planting out in early June, starting them under cloches in colder areas. The aim is to grow them quickly, so they must never go short of water – but water round the plants, not over them, or they will rot.

Harvesting. Pick the courgettes when they are about 4in (10cm) long. Keep picking or they will stop producing.

Capsicums

These sweet peppers are not easy to grow. Even in mild areas they will need protecting with tall cloches in the early stages. In colder areas they are usually grown in pots or growing bags in a greenhouse. The variety Canape F_1 is good for outdoors and New Ace F_1, for indoors.

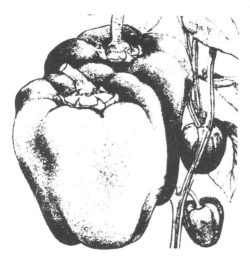

GROWING CAPSICUMS

For plants to be grown in a greenhouse, sow seeds, in late February, one seed in each peat pot. Keep in a propagator at 60°F (16°C). When the first true leaves appear, transfer to 4in (10cm) pots. Move into loam compost in 8in (20cm) pots in late May. In warm areas they will not need artificial heat beyond then.

For plants to be grown outside, sow seeds in March. Harden them off to go outside in early June under cloches, (put in place two weeks in advance). Plant 18in (45cm) apart in a single row. Support the plants.

Harvesting. Pick the capsicums when they are green and glossy.

Aubergines

Aubergines, another tropical vegetable fruit, are also known as eggplants because of their shape. They can be grown outdoors in warm areas given a good summer, a sheltered sunny position – for example, against a south-facing wall – and a rich fertile soil. They can also be raised on a sunny patio in pots, as they are in the greenhouse. But they are harder to grow than peppers and are best raised under tall cloches or in pots in a greenhouse. The variety Long Purple has been around for some time, but there are newer F_1 hybrids such as the prolific Black Enorma, Black Prince, Dusky and Moneymaker.

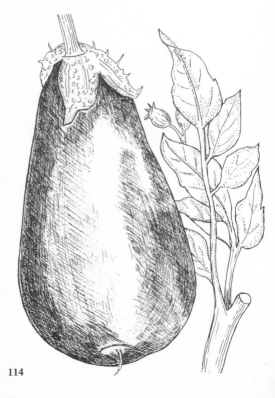

114

GROWING AUBERGINES

Whether they are to grow outdoors or inside, the seedlings must be raised in heat, 60-65°F (16-18°C). For greenhouse plants, sow seeds in February, two to each peat pot; they may take two to three weeks to germinate. Keep the stronger seedling. Move it to a larger pot of loam-based compost and later into a 9in (23cm) pot. Transfer to a heated greenhouse in April or an unheated greenhouse early in May.

For outdoor plants, sow seeds in late March and harden off before planting out under tall cloches in late May, 24in (60cm) apart.

Remove the growing tip when the plants are 10in (25cm) high. After four fruits have set, remove the side shoots and the rest of the flowers. Keep the soil moist and apply liquid fertilizer when the fruits begin to swell.

Harvesting. From August onwards. Pick the fruits when they are plump and ripe and the bloom is still on them. If they are left too long on the plant they will grow bitter.

Pests and diseases of tomatoes, aubergines and capsicums

Tomatoes, especially those grown in greenhouses, can suffer from many pests and diseases. But thoroughly clean greenhouses and a fertile soil will help in escaping them. Aubergines and capsicums are also liable to be affected, but often escape. Of the virus diseases, the most common is tomato mosaic (yellow mottling of the leaves and stunted growth). There is no cure. Destroy the diseased plants, and after handling them wash your hands thoroughly before touching other plants or you will pass on the infection. Some viruses are common to tomatoes and tobacco, so smokers would be well advised not to handle tomato plants straight away after smoking.

However, aphids are the main carriers of virus diseases, so the first defence is to destroy them. Spray with derris.

Outdoor tomatoes may be ruined by blight in wet seasons. Nothing can be done once the disease has taken hold, but to help to prevent it spray with a copper fungicide when most of the plants have had their growing tips pinched out.

Pests and diseases of cucumbers and marrows

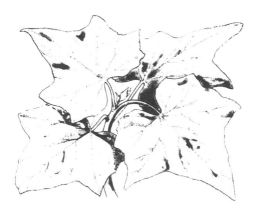

Cucumbers, and marrows even more, are susceptible to cucumber mosaic virus, indicated by yellow mottling of the leaves and fruits which die before they develop. There is no cure; burn infected plants. Greenfly carry the virus. Destroy them.

Mildew often attacks marrows in the autumn, usually when the soil is dry and the air humid. It shows as white powdery patches on leaves and stems. One step that can be taken to prevent it is to make sure that the marrow beds never get dry.

117

IN THE KITCHEN

There are few things more rewarding
than harvesting the vegetables that you
have grown in your kitchen garden.
Equally satisfying is the task of preparing and cooking them so that their taste
is enhanced, texture preserved and nutrients not lost.

The recipes that follow offer variety
with simplicity – delicious rewards for
your labours in the garden.

Salad Plants

Salad plants are interchangeable in most
recipes. They also mix well in composite
salads adding diversity in colour, texture
and flavour.

CAESAR SALAD

SERVES SIX
Olive oil
3 garlic cloves
*4 large, thick slices of bread, trimmed
    and cut into ½-inch (1 cm) cubes*
*2 cos lettuces, washed, dried and
    chilled*
1 egg
Juice of 1 lemon
16 anchovy fillets, cut into pieces
2 oz (60 g) Parmesan cheese, grated
Salt and pepper

Heat 4 tablespoons of olive oil in a frying
pan with 2 crushed garlic cloves. Fry the
bread cubes until crisp and golden on all
118 sides, adding more oil as needed. Drain the

croûtons thoroughly on kitchen paper. Crush the remaining garlic clove and rub it around a salad bowl.

Tear the lettuce in bite-size pieces into the salad bowl. Add 8 tablespoons olive oil and toss until every leaf is thoroughly coated. Cook the egg in boiling water for 1 minute. Break it over the lettuce, add the lemon juice, anchovies, cheese, and salt and pepper to taste.

Toss gently until well mixed. Adjust seasoning. Add the croûtons, toss again and serve immediately, while the croûtons are still crisp.

LETTUCE SALAD WITH HOT BACON DRESSING

SERVES FOUR
1 garlic clove, halved
1 large cos lettuce, washed and dried
4 thick slices streaky bacon, diced
1 teaspoon butter
1 tablespoon wine vinegar
1 hard-boiled egg, chopped
2 tablespoons finely chopped parsley
Salt and pepper

Rub a warmed salad bowl with the garlic. Tear the lettuce into the bowl in bite-size pieces. Set aside.

Fry the bacon gently in the butter for 10 minutes, or until the fat runs, and pour over the greens. Add the vinegar to the pan, swirl to heat it and sprinkle over the salad in the bowl.

Toss the salad thoroughly. Add the chopped egg, parsley and salt and pepper to taste. Toss again and serve.

CHICORY AND ORANGE SALAD

SERVES FOUR

1 tablespoon lemon juice
Salt and pepper
French mustard
Cayenne pepper or Tabasco sauce
1 teaspoon honey
3 tablespoons olive oil
1 orange, peeled and sliced
*4 heads chicory, prepared, washed
   and thinly sliced crosswise*
12 black olives, to garnish

In a salad bowl, mix the lemon juice with a little salt, pepper, mustard, cayenne or Tabasco and the honey. Beat in the oil until the dressing is smooth and creamy. Taste and add more lemon juice, seasoning or honey if necessary. Set aside.

Cut the orange slices into quarters. Put the orange and chicory into the salad bowl. Toss gently but well. Serve immediately, garnished with black olives.

Brassicas

One thing most of the numerous members of the cabbage family have in common is that they taste wonderful if lightly cooked – steamed, simmered or stir-fried – and dreadful if boiled to death.

SWEDISH RED CABBAGE

SERVES EIGHT
1 red cabbage, about 3 lb (1½ kg),
*   finely shredded*
2 oz (60 g) fat salt pork, diced
2 Spanish onions, thinly sliced
4 tablespoons brown sugar
½ lb (¼ kg) tart dessert apples,
*   peeled, cored and chopped*
¼ pint (125 ml) chicken stock
¼ pint (125 ml) red wine
3 tablespoons wine or cider vinegar
Salt and pepper
1 small raw beetroot, coarsely grated

Put the cabbage in a large bowl and pour over enough boiling water to cover.

In a large heavy casserole, sauté the salt pork until the fat runs. Add the onions and fry over moderate heat until soft and transparent. Stir in the sugar and continue to fry gently until the onions are caramelized and a rich golden colour. Take great care not to let the sugar burn.

Drain the cabbage thoroughly. Add it to the casserole, together with the apples, stock, wine and vinegar. Mix well. Season generously with salt and pepper. Cover tightly and cook gently for 1½ hours, stirring occasionally.

Mix in the beetroot – this transforms the colour – and continue to cook for 30 minutes longer. Correct seasoning and serve very hot.

CABBAGE QUICHE

SERVES FOUR AS A MAIN DISH

*Rich shortcrust pastry made with ¹/₂
  lb (¹/₄ kg) flour*
1 lb (¹/₂ kg) finely shredded cabbage
¹/₄ lb (120 g) butter
3 eggs
*¹/₂ pint (250 ml) single cream and
  milk, mixed*
*4 tablespoons freshly grated Gruyère
  cheese*
*3 tablespoons freshly grated Parme-
  san cheese*
Salt and pepper
Freshly grated nutmeg

Preheat the oven to 425°F (220°C, Gas Mark
7). Roll out the pastry and line a 9-inch (22
cm) tart tin with a removable base. Line the
pastry with greaseproof paper or foil, fill
with dried beans and bake 'blind' for 15
minutes. Remove the paper and beans, and
let the base dry out for a further 5 minutes in
the oven.

Reduce the oven temperature to 350°F
(180°C, Gas Mark 4).

Meanwhile, put the cabbage in a colander
and slowly pour a kettle of boiling water
over it. Shake off excess moisture.

In a large, heavy saucepan melt the
butter. Add the cabbage, cover tightly and
cook over moderate heat until the cabbage is
soft and golden. Shake the pan occasionally
to prevent the cabbage burning. The cooking time will depend on the type of cabbage
used, but firm white cabbage takes about 30
minutes. Remove the pan from the heat.

In a small bowl, beat the eggs with the
cream and milk. Let the cabbage cool
slightly, then stir in the egg mixture and 2
tablespoons each of the Gruyère and Parmesan. Add salt, pepper and nutmeg to taste.

Spoon the mixture into the pastry shell.
Sprinkle the remaining cheese over the top.

Put the quiche in the oven and bake for 30 minutes, or until the filling is set and a rich golden colour. Remove the quiche from the oven and leave it to settle. Serve warm.

CREAM OF CAULIFLOWER SOUP

SERVES FOUR TO SIX
1 medium-sized cauliflower
1 pint (500 ml) milk
Salt and pepper
1 1/2 pints (750 ml) chicken stock
1 oz (30 g) butter
2 tablespoons flour
Sharp Cheddar cheese, grated

Cut off a handful of tiny florets no bigger than daisy heads from the cauliflower. Bring 1/4 pint (125 ml) of the milk to the boil with 1/4 pint (125 ml) of water and a pinch of salt. Add the florets and poach for a few minutes, until cooked but still very firm. Drain them, reserving the liquor, and set aside.

Chop the remainder of the cauliflower into chunks. Put in a pan with 1 pint (500 ml) of the chicken stock, the rest of the milk and the reserved cauliflower liquor. Bring to the boil and cook, covered, until the cauliflower is soft. Purée the contents of the pan.

In another pan melt the butter. Blend in the flour and stir over low heat for 1 minute. Gradually stir in the remaining stock to make a smooth sauce. Add the puréed cauliflower mixture and bring to the boil. Season to taste with salt and pepper and simmer for 5 minutes.

Taste the soup. If it seems too bland, stir in 2 or 3 tablespoons of cheese. Add the poached florets and heat them through. Serve the soup with a bowl of cheese for sprinkling over each portion.

RECIPES

STUFFED KOHLRABI

SERVES SIX
6 fist-sized kohlrabi
Salt
Butter
1 small onion, finely chopped
1 garlic clove, crushed
1/2 lb (1/4 kg) lean pork, minced
1 egg, lightly beaten
1 teaspoon tomato concentrate
3 oz (90 g) trimmed brown bread,
  soaked in milk
Pepper
3/4 pint (375 ml) chicken stock
1 oz (30 g) flour
Juice of 1/2 lemon
Finely chopped parsley, to garnish

Trim the kohlrabi, cutting off the stalks and shaving the bases so that each bulb will sit steadily. Peel the kohlrabi thinly. Cut a slice off the tops and scoop out the centres to make cups about 1/3 inch (1 cm) thick. Finely chop half of the scooped-out flesh and put it aside.

Place a steamer over a pan of simmering water. Arrange the kohlrabi cups upside down in the steamer. Sprinkle them with salt. Cover the pan and steam for 10 minutes.

Preheat the oven to 375°F (190°C, Gas Mark 5).

Prepare the stuffing. In a saucepan, heat 1 ounce (30 g) of butter. Add the onion, garlic and chopped kohlrabi and fry, stirring occasionally, until softened and lightly coloured. Remove the pan from the heat. Mix in the pork, egg and tomato concentrate. Squeeze the bread dry. Crumble it into the pan and mix it in well. Season to taste with salt and pepper.

Arrange the steamed kohlrabi cups side by side in a buttered baking dish. Put a flake of butter in the bottom of each cup and stuff

124

them with the meat mixture. Pour ½ pint (250 ml) of the stock around the kohlrabi. Cover the dish loosely with foil and bake for 20 minutes. Baste with the cooking juices and bake for a further 15 minutes until the kohlrabi are tender and the stuffing is cooked through.

With a slotted spoon, transfer the kohlrabi to a hot serving dish. Keep hot.

Melt 1 ounce (30 g) of butter in a small saucepan. Blend in the flour and stir over low heat for about 4 minutes to make a nutty brown *roux*. Gradually blend in the remaining stock. Add the juices left in the baking dish and a little lemon juice to taste. Bring the sauce to the boil and simmer for 2 minutes. Correct the seasoning. Spoon the sauce over the kohlrabi, garnish with parsley and serve.

PURÉED BRUSSELS SPROUTS

Puréed sprouts can also be used as a base for making a soufflé – 1 pound (½ kg) of purée will require 3 egg yolks and 4 egg whites.

SERVES FOUR TO SIX
1½ lb (¾ kg) Brussels sprouts
¼ pint (125 ml) single cream
½ lb (¼ kg) puréed potatoes
2 oz (60 g) butter, melted
Salt and pepper
Nutmeg

Poach the sprouts in salted water for 5 minutes. Drain well.

Purée the sprouts with the cream in an electric blender. Pour the purée into a large bowl. Add the puréed potato and the butter and beat well until the mixture is light and fluffy. Season to taste with salt, pepper and a grating of nutmeg.

Return the purée to the pan and reheat gently, adding more cream if necessary.

BROCCOLI SICILIAN STYLE

SERVES SIX

2 tablespoons olive oil
1 Spanish onion, finely chopped
12 black olives, pitted and sliced
6 anchovy fillets, chopped, and the
    can oil reserved
2 lb (1 kg) fresh broccoli
1/4 pint (125 ml) chicken stock
1/4 pint (125 ml) red wine
Pepper
1 teaspoon butter
1 teaspoon flour
Salt

Heat the olive oil in a large, flameproof casserole. Stir in the onion, olives and anchovy fillets. Simmer gently, uncovered, for 5 minutes.

Add the broccoli, turning the pieces over to coat them with the oil. Add the stock and wine. Sprinkle with 1 tablespoon of the oil drained from the can of anchovy fillets and season with a generous grinding of pepper. Cover the casserole and cook over moderate heat, stirring occasionally, for 15 minutes.

When the broccoli is tender, uncover the pan and continue simmering for 3 minutes longer. Using a slotted spoon, transfer the broccoli to a serving dish and keep hot.

Thicken the sauce in the pan with a *beurre manié* made by mashing the butter and flour to a smooth paste and stirring it in in small pieces. Add salt if necessary. Stir the sauce until it comes to the boil. Pour it over the broccoli and serve.

126

Spinach

Spinach in its many guises is a wonderful vegetable. It can be used in salads and soups, pastries and pies of all kinds, soufflés, omelettes, gratins and creams, proving its versatility in all but the sweet course.

CREAMED SPINACH, POLISH STYLE

SERVES FOUR
2 oz (60 g) butter
1 large Spanish onion, finely chopped
2 tablespoons flour
3 lb (1½ kg) fresh spinach, cooked
  and chopped
½ pint (250 ml) creamy milk
1 tablespoon tomato concentrate
  (optional)
Sugar
Salt and pepper
Nutmeg
Lemon juice
4 eggs, poached

GARNISH
4 rashers bacon, fried
Triangular croûtons

Melt the butter in a large pan. Add the onion and cook, stirring, until soft and golden. Add the flour and stir over low heat for 2 to 3 minutes to make a golden *roux*. Blend in the spinach. Gradually stir in the milk. Beat in the tomato concentrate, if used, and add a generous pinch of sugar to taste.

Bring the mixture to simmering point. Partly cover the pan and cook over low heat for about 20 minutes, stirring frequently.

Season with salt, pepper, nutmeg and lemon juice to taste. Continue to simmer gently for a further 10 minutes. Serve topped with the poached eggs and garnished with the bacon and croûtons.

SPINACH CUTLETS

SERVES FOUR
1 oz (30 g) butter
1 medium-sized onion, finely chopped
2 lb (1 kg) fresh spinach, cooked and
*   finely chopped or minced*
1 large egg
Fine dry breadcrumbs
Salt and pepper
Nutmeg
Oil or bacon fat, for frying

Melt the butter in a large pan. Add the onion
and cook gently until soft and lightly coloured. Remove the pan from the heat and
stir in the spinach, egg and 2 ounces (60 g)
breadcrumbs. Mix well and season to taste
with salt, pepper and nutmeg.

Shape the mixture into eight flat, oval
cakes and coat them with dry breadcrumbs.
Fry the cakes in hot oil or bacon fat on both
sides until the crumbs are golden and the
cutlets are heated through.

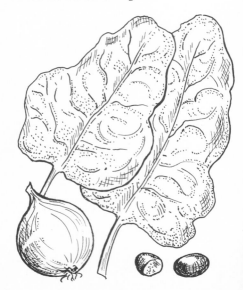

Stalks and Shoots

Stalks and shoots are a mixed bunch –
asparagus and artichokes, celery, Florence
fennel and rhubarb. To all appearances they
have little in common except, perhaps, that
most of them have enjoyed, at one stage or
another in their history, a reputation as
aphrodisiacs.

ASPARAGUS WITH SCRAMBLED EGGS

Serve on hot toast or in little pastry cases.

SERVES TWO TO THREE
6 eggs
2 tablespoons double cream
Salt and pepper
1 oz (30 g) butter
12 asparagus spears, cooked and
  sliced
2 tablespoons grated Parmesan
  cheese

In a bowl, beat the eggs and the cream
together with a fork until just mixed. Season
to taste with salt and pepper.

Melt the butter in a non-stick saucepan.
Add the asparagus and cook gently, stirring,
for 1 minute. Pour in the egg mixture and,
stirring constantly, cook over the lowest
possible heat until the eggs begin to set in
creamy curds. Stir in the cheese and, as soon
as the eggs have set to the right consistency,
remove the pan from the heat and serve.

BAKED ASPARAGUS WITH PASTA

SERVES FOUR

1/2 lb (1/4 kg) macaroni
1/2 lb (1/4 kg) fresh or frozen
    asparagus
1/2 pint (250 ml) hot single cream
Salt and pepper
2 eggs, beaten
5 tablespoons freshly grated
    Parmesan cheese
1 tablespoon butter

Boil the macaroni in a large pan of salted water, following the timing recommended on the packet.

Meanwhile, cut the asparagus into 3/4-inch (2 cm) lengths and parboil in just enough salted water to cover until half done – 6 to 8 minutes for fresh asparagus, only 4 minutes for frozen.

Preheat the oven to 400°F (200°C, Gas Mark 6).

Drain the asparagus in a strainer held over the pot of boiling macaroni. Then drop the asparagus into a pan containing the hot cream and simmer for 2 minutes. Season to taste with salt and pepper. Cover and put aside.

Drain the macaroni. Return it to the pan and stir over low heat for a minute or two to evaporate any remaining moisture. Cool slightly. Then carefully mix in the asparagus and cream, followed by the eggs and 3 tablespoons of grated Parmesan.

Pour the mixture into a well-buttered baking dish. Sprinkle with the remaining Parmesan and dot with butter.

Bake for 20 to 25 minutes, or until set and the top golden and bubbling. Serve hot.

BAKED STUFFED ARTICHOKES

SERVES SIX
6 artichokes, chokes removed
Lemon juice
Salt
3 oz (90 g) fresh white breadcrumbs
1 medium-sized onion, finely chopped
6 anchovy fillets, finely chopped
3 tablespoons finely chopped parsley
2 tablespoons chopped capers
Olive oil
¾ pint (375 ml) chicken stock

Leave the artichokes to soak in acidulated water for 30 minutes. Parboil them in salted water for 10 minutes and drain thoroughly.

Preheat the oven to 375°F (190°C, Gas Mark 5).

To make the stuffing, mix the breadcrumbs, onion, anchovies, parsley and capers together. Add 2 tablespoons of olive oil. Season generously with pepper (no salt because of the anchovies) and mix lightly with a fork.

Fill the centres of the artichokes with the stuffing. If there is any filling left stuff it between the leaves, using a spoon.

Select a deep baking dish just large enough to hold the artichokes side by side. Brush it with oil. Brush each artichoke with oil and sprinkle a little of it over the stuffing in the centre. Arrange the artichokes in the baking dish. Add the stock and bake for 1 hour, or until a leaf from near the base can easily be pulled out. Baste regularly with the stock, which should almost all have been absorbed by the end of the cooking time. Serve hot.

STIR-FRIED CELERY WITH SESAME SAUCE

If sesame paste is not available substitute smooth peanut butter, either alone or mixed with sesame oil (2 tablespoons peanut butter, 1 tablespoon sesame oil).

SERVES FOUR
1 lb (½ kg) celery
3 tablespoons vegetable oil
1 small onion, finely chopped
2 garlic cloves, crushed
½-inch (1 cm) piece fresh root ginger,
    peeled and shredded
Salt
1 tablespoon dry sherry
1½ tablespoon soy sauce
1 teaspoon sugar

SESAME SAUCE
5 tablespoons sesame paste
3 tablespoons light stock
2 tablespoons soy sauce
2 tablespoons wine vinegar
2 teaspoons sugar
Chilli sauce
2 garlic cloves, crushed

First prepare the sesame sauce. In a saucepan combine the sesame paste with the stock, soy sauce and vinegar. Add the sugar, and chilli sauce to taste. Cook over low heat, stirring constantly, for 3 minutes. Remove the pan from the heat and stir in the garlic.

Cut the celery stalks diagonally in 2-inch (5 cm) pieces. Heat the oil in a large frying-pan. Add the onion, garlic and ginger and fry, stirring constantly, for 1 minute. Add the celery and salt to taste. Turn the celery in the pan until it is well coated with the oil. Stir in the sherry, soy sauce and sugar. Continue to cook for 2 to 3 minutes.

Serve with the reheated sesame sauce in a separate bowl.

RHUBARB KISIEL

Serve with a vanilla custard sauce or single cream.

SERVES FOUR
1 lb (½ kg) rhubarb, cut into chunks
6 oz (180 g) sugar
Juice of 1 large orange
4 tablespoons cornflour

Put the rhubarb in an enamelled pan with the sugar and the orange juice made up to ½ pint (250 ml) with water. Cover tightly and cook over low heat for 10 minutes, or until the rhubarb has disintegrated. Mash the rhubarb and mix it with the juices.

Blend the cornflour to a smooth paste with 6 tablespoons of cold water. Stir it into the hot rhubarb purée. Bring to the boil and cook over low heat, stirring constantly, for 4 minutes, or until the mixture is thick and has lost its floury opaqueness.

Divide between four dishes or pour into a decorative mould rinsed out with cold water. Turn out and serve very cold.

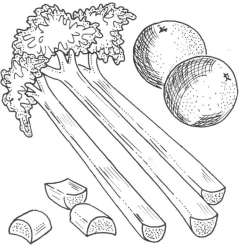

Pods and Seeds

Pods and seeds are an important source of nourishment for they provide more protein and energy than most other vegetables. Fresh or dried they make a tasty and healthy contribution to our diet.

CORN CHOWDER

SERVES FOUR TO SIX
*1 lb (½ kg) potatoes, peeled and
   diced*
2 oz (60 g) fat salt pork, diced
1 Spanish onion, coarsely chopped
1 tablespoon flour
½ pint (250 ml) milk
¾ pint (375 ml) chicken stock
½ lb (¼ kg) sweet corn kernels
½ pint (250 ml) single cream
*½ sweet green pepper, cored, seeded
   and finely chopped*
Salt and pepper
Paprika

Parboil the potatoes in salted water for 5 minutes. Drain thoroughly and set aside.

In a large saucepan, fry the salt pork until the fat runs. Add the onion and fry gently, stirring frequently, until soft and lightly coloured. Sprinkle with the flour and stir over low heat for 1 minute. Gradually stir in the milk. Then add the stock, corn kernels and potatoes and bring to the boil, stirring. Reduce the heat, cover the pan and simmer gently for 7 to 10 minutes, or until the corn and the potatoes are tender.

Stir in the cream and the pepper. Season to taste with salt, pepper and a pinch of paprika. Bring the soup back to boiling point and serve.

RICE WITH PEAS

This Italian dish may also be served as a
soup. Just thin the mixture down with more
stock. Leave out the final ounce of butter
and serve garnished with Parmesan and
parsley.

SERVES SIX TO EIGHT
2 tablespoons olive oil
3 oz (90 g) butter
*4 thick slices fat unsmoked bacon or
    ham, finely diced*
1 large, mild onion, finely chopped
¾ lb (360 g) Italian rice
*2 to 3 pints (1 to 1½ litres) chicken
    stock, boiling*
2 lb (1 kg) tiny, fresh green peas
*2 oz (60 g) freshly grated Parmesan
    cheese*
Salt and pepper
2 tablespoons finely chopped parsley

Heat the oil and 2 ounces (60 g) of the butter
in a large, heavy pan. Add the bacon or ham
and onion and fry over low heat until the
onion is soft and lightly coloured. Stir in the
rice. Add ¾ pint (375 ml) of the boiling
stock and simmer gently, uncovered, stirring frequently, until most of the stock has
been absorbed.

Using a large fork, gently mix in the peas.
Pour in 1¼ pints (625 ml) of stock and
continue to simmer over low heat for 15
minutes, or until both the peas and rice are
tender and most of the stock has been
absorbed.

Remove the pan from the heat. Add the
remaining butter and 1 ounce (30 g) of the
grated Parmesan. Mix gently and season to
taste. Cover and set aside for 5 to 10 minutes
to allow the rice to absorb any excess stock.
Serve sprinkled with the remaining Parmesan mixed with the parsley.

FRENCH BEANS IN MUSHROOM CREAM SAUCE

SERVES FOUR
1 lb (½ kg) young French beans
2 oz (60 g) butter
1 small, mild onion, finely chopped
¼ lb (120 g) button mushrooms, sliced
Lemon juice
6 tablespoons single cream
Salt and pepper

Drop the beans into a large pan of boiling salted water and cook them briskly for 5 minutes, or until tender but still crisp.

Meanwhile, melt the butter in a large, wide pan and fry the onion gently until soft and golden. Add the mushrooms. Squeeze a little lemon juice over them to prevent them discolouring and cook gently for 3 to 5 minutes, or until they are golden and have softened slightly.

Drain the beans thoroughly and mix them with the onion and mushrooms. Add the cream and season to taste with salt and pepper. Cook over low heat, stirring gently, until the sauce comes to simmering point; then let it bubble for about 3 minutes until it is reduced to a thick coating consistency.

RUNNER BEANS GREEK STYLE

This dish can be served in the Greek style –
lukewarm with crusty bread to soak up the
sauce.

SERVES FOUR TO SIX
2 lb (1 kg) runner beans
Salt
1 large, mild onion, finely chopped
*4 large, ripe tomatoes, peeled and
    chopped*
6 tablespoons finely chopped parsley
6 tablespoons olive oil
2 teaspoons sugar
Pepper

String the beans and slice them lengthwise
into thin strips. Put the beans in a colander
and sprinkle them generously with salt. Rub
the salt gently into the beans. Set aside for 1
hour to allow the beans to wilt and soften.

Rinse the beans thoroughly under cold
running water, then shake off as much
moisture as possible.

In a heavy pan, combine the beans with
the onion, tomatoes, parsley and olive oil.
Sprinkle with the sugar and add a generous
grinding of pepper. Add just enough boiling
water to cover. Bring to simmering point,
partially cover the pan and cook gently for
30 minutes, or until the beans are tender and
the sauce is thick. Remove the pan from the
heat and set aside to cool.

Adjust the seasoning and serve lukewarm
or cold.

BROAD BEANS WITH BACON

SERVES FOUR TO SIX
1 oz (30 g) butter
4 slices unsmoked bacon, diced
1 medium-sized onion, finely chopped
1 lb (½ kg) shelled baby broad beans
¼ pint (125 ml) stock or water
Salt and pepper

Melt the butter in a pan. Add the bacon and
onion and fry until the onion is soft but not
coloured. Stir in the beans. Add the stock or
water and bring to the boil. Cover and cook
over moderate heat for 6 to 8 minutes or
until the beans are soft but not mushy.

If there is too much liquid left by the time
the beans are ready, boil them briskly,
uncovered, for 1 to 2 minutes to evaporate
the excess moisture.

CHINESE SNOW PEAS

SERVES FOUR
1 lb (½ kg) mangetout peas
2 tablespoons vegetable oil
½ chicken stock cube
Salt
½ oz (15 g) lard

Wash and drain the *mangetout* peas. Top,
tail and string them as you would green
beans and pat them dry.

Heat the oil in a wok. Add the *mangetout*
and stir over low heat for 30 seconds.
Crumble the stock cube and sprinkle a little
salt over the pods. Add 4 tablespoons of hot
water and stir-fry for 30 seconds longer.

Remove the pan from the heat. Stir and
turn the pea pods for 1 minute. Return to
moderate heat and cook, stirring, until most
of the liquid has evaporated.

Add the lard in small pieces and stir over
low heat until it has melted.

The Onion Family

The onion family have been regarded as a food and a flavouring probably longer than any other cultivated vegetables. Indeed, the very thought of cooking without them is almost as absurd as trying to get by without seasoning.

SWEET AND SOUR ONIONS

This delicious regional Italian dish can be served either hot or cold, as part of a mixed *hors d'oeuvre* or as an accompaniment to roast meat or chicken.

SERVES FOUR
3 tablespoons olive oil
1¹/₂ lb (³/₄ kg) button onions, peeled
3 tablespoons white wine
3 tablespoons wine vinegar
2 tablespoons soft brown sugar
2 tablespoons pine nuts
2 tablespoons raisins
Salt and pepper
Finely chopped parsley, to garnish

Heat the oil in a large frying-pan. Add the onions and cook over a moderate heat, shaking the pan occasionally, until the onions begin to brown. Add the wine, vinegar, sugar, pine nuts and raisins. Season with salt and pepper. Reduce the heat, cover the pan and simmer until the sauce has become syrupy and the onions are tender. Correct the seasoning and serve garnished with the chopped parsley.

ONIONS IN MADEIRA CREAM

SERVES FOUR TO SIX
1/4 lb (120 g) butter
4 large, mild onions, thickly sliced
1/4 pint (125 ml) Madeira
Salt and pepper
4 tablespoons double cream
4 tablespoons finely chopped parsley

Melt the butter in a wide, heavy pan. Add the onion slices and turn them thoroughly in the butter. Cover the pan and cook over very low heat for 10 minutes, shaking the pan occasionally.

Uncover the pan, increase the heat slightly and stir in the Madeira. Continue to cook, stirring frequently, until the Madeira has evaporated and the onions are soft and lightly caramelized.

Season to taste with salt and pepper. Stir in the cream and parsley and bring to the boil. Simmer for 1 minute. Serve hot.

ONION TART

SERVES SIX TO EIGHT
3 oz (90 g) butter
1 1/2 lb (3/4 kg) large onions, thinly sliced
2 tablespoons finely chopped parsley
2 teaspoons dried basil
Rich shortcrust pastry made with 1/2 lb (1/4 kg) flour
1/2 pint (250 ml) single cream
3 large eggs
2 oz (60 g) Gruyère cheese, grated
Salt and pepper

TOPPING
1 oz (30 g) Gruyère cheese, grated
4 tablespoons fresh white breadcrumbs

Melt the butter in a saucepan. Add the onions and cook gently, covered, for 15 minutes. Stir frequently. When the onions are limp, uncover the pan and continue to fry gently for 15 to 20 minutes, or until they become very soft without colouring. Remove from the heat and stir in the herbs.

Preheat the oven to 425°F (220°C, Gas Mark 7).

Roll the pastry out and line a 10-inch (25 cm) tart tin with a removable base. Prick the pastry case with a fork and line it with greaseproof paper or foil. Fill the case with dried beans and bake 'blind' for 15 minutes. Remove the beans and paper and return the pastry case to the oven for 5 minutes. Remove from the oven and set aside.

Reduce the oven temperature to 375°F (190°C, Gas Mark 5). Heat a baking sheet in the oven.

Beat the cream lightly with the eggs and cheese and mix it into the onion mixture. Season with salt and pepper.

Put the pastry case on the hot baking sheet and pour in the filling. Mix the grated Gruyère with the breadcrumbs and sprinkle over the top.

Bake the tart for 35 minutes, or until the filling is puffed and set.

LEEKS WITH TOMATOES AND OLIVES

SERVES FOUR
2 lb (1 kg) trimmed leeks
3 tablespoons olive oil
4 large tomatoes, halved
2 oz (60 g) black olives, pitted
Juice of 1 lemon
Rind of 1/2 lemon, in one piece
Salt and pepper

Cut the leeks into 1-inch (2 cm) lengths. Heat the oil in a large, deep frying-pan. Add the leeks, cover the pan and cook slowly for about 10 minutes, stirring occasionally.

Add the tomatoes, olives, half of the lemon juice, the lemon rind and salt and pepper to taste. Simmer, covered, for a further 10 minutes.

Remove and discard the lemon rind and add the remaining lemon juice. Adjust the seasoning. Serve hot or cold.

VICHYSSOISE

SERVES FOUR TO SIX
2 oz (60 g) butter
6 large leeks, white part only, thickly
    sliced
1 1/2 lb (3/4 kg) potatoes, peeled and
    thickly sliced
2 pints (1 litre) chicken stock
Salt and pepper
Grated nutmeg
3/4 pint (375 ml) single cream
Chopped chives, to garnish

Melt the butter in a large saucepan. Add the leeks, cover the pan and simmer for 15 minutes. Turn the leeks over to make sure they soften without changing colour. Add the potatoes, pour in the stock and simmer gently, with the lid half on, for a further 15 to 20 minutes, or until the vegetables have begun to disintegrate. Purée the soup. Season with salt, pepper and nutmeg to taste.

If the soup is to be served cold, let it cool before diluting it with the cream. If it is to be served hot, add the cream and bring to boiling point. Garnish with chopped chives.

GARLIC BREAD

SERVES FOUR
1 long French loaf
¼ lb (120 g) butter, softened
2 plump garlic cloves, crushed
1 tablespoon finely chopped parsley
Sea salt, and pepper

Preheat the oven to 350°F (180°C, Gas Mark 4).

Slice the loaf diagonally at 1½-inch (4 cm) intervals to within a ¼ inch (½ cm) of the base. Pound the butter with the garlic and parsley. Mix in salt and pepper to taste.

Carefully easing the slices of bread apart, spread each one with the garlic butter. Wrap the loaf tightly in foil and bake it for about 20 minutes, or until the butter has melted and the bread is hot and crusty.

Roots and Tubers

The great advantage of roots and tubers used to be that, with few exceptions, they could be harvested and stored in a cellar to tide the household over the winter months. But even today, with so many imported vegetables bringing variety to winter diets, roots and tubers still provide a cheap and nourishing staple.

TURNIPS IN CREAM

SERVES SIX

2 lb (1 kg) baby turnips, peeled
1/4 pint (125 ml) double cream
5 tablespoons chicken stock
1/2 teaspoon dried basil
1/4 teaspoon sugar
Salt and pepper
1 teaspoon cornflour
2 tablespoons finely chopped parsley

Put the turnips in a large, heavy pan. Blend the cream with the chicken stock and pour over the turnips. Add the basil, sugar, and salt and pepper to taste. Mix well and bring to simmering point over low heat. Cover the pan tightly and cook gently for about 20 minutes, or until the turnips can be easily pierced with a sharp fork or skewer.

Remove the pan from the heat and, with a slotted spoon, transfer the turnips to a heated serving dish. Keep hot.

Blend the cornflour to a smooth paste with 3 tablespoons of cold water and stir into the liquid in the pan. Return the pan to the heat and cook, stirring, until the sauce comes to simmering point and thickens slightly. Taste and correct the seasoning if necessary.

Pour the sauce over the turnips. Sprinkle with parsley and serve.

BUTTERED CARROTS AND MUSHROOMS

SERVES FOUR
1 lb (½ kg) carrots, sliced
1½ oz (45 g) butter
1 tablespoon oil
1 small onion, finely chopped
1 garlic clove, crushed ·
¼ lb (120 g) button mushrooms,
   thickly sliced
1 whole cardamom pod
Pinch of dried rosemary
Salt and pepper

Steam the carrots or simmer in salted water for 5 minutes, or until the slices are barely tender. Drain well.

While the carrots are cooking, heat the butter and oil in another pan. Add the onion and garlic and fry, stirring constantly, until the onion is soft and lightly coloured. Add the mushrooms and fry, stirring, for 2 to 3 minutes until they are golden.

Mix in the carrots, cardamom pod, rosemary and salt and pepper to taste. Mix well. Cover the pan tightly and cook over very low heat for 15 minutes to develop and blend the flavours.

GLAZED PARSNIPS

SERVES FOUR
8 parsnips
2 oz (60 g) butter
2 tablespoons light-brown sugar
Juice of 1 large orange
2 tablespoons lemon juice
Generous pinch nutmeg or mace
Salt and pepper

Scrub the parsnips with a stiff brush. Trim them top and bottom, and boil in salted water until barely tender – about 12 minutes. Drain them thoroughly and allow to cool. Peel them and slice off the thin root ends, leaving them in one or two pieces. Slice the thicker ends in half lengthwise.

Put the butter, sugar, orange juice and lemon juice into a wide, heavy pan. Stir over low heat. When the butter has melted and the sugar dissolved, stir in the nutmeg or mace.

Put the pieces of parsnip in the pan, turning them to coat them with the buttery juices. Season with salt and a grinding of pepper. Cook over low heat, partially covered, until the parsnips are glazed on all sides and have absorbed the juices. Serve hot.

HARVARD BEETS

SERVES FOUR TO SIX
1½ lb (¾ kg) beetroot, cooked
2½ oz (75 g) sugar
1 tablespoon cornflour
6 tablespoons mild wine or cider vinegar
Salt
1 oz (30 g) butter

Trim the beetroots, rub off their skins and
146 slice them thinly.

In a pan blend the sugar and cornflour with the vinegar. Cook over low heat, stirring constantly, until the mixture comes to the boil and thickens.

Carefully mix the prepared beetroots into the sauce. Season to taste with salt and cook gently, stirring occasionally, for 25 to 30 minutes, until the beetroots are hot and the sauce is a deep red.

Add the butter, stirring until it has melted. Serve immediately.

CELERIAC AND HAM SALAD

SERVES FOUR
¾ lb (360 g) celeriac root, scrubbed
1 egg yolk
2 teaspoons Dijon mustard
2 teaspoons tarragon vinegar
8 tablespoons olive oil
Salt and pepper
¼ lb (120 g) lean cooked ham, cubed
2 medium-sized carrots, coarsely
  grated
2 tablespoons finely chopped parsley
Lettuce leaves, to garnish

Put the celeriac into a large pan of rapidly boiling salted water and boil for 30 minutes. The celeriac should still feel very firm when pierced with a skewer.

While the celeriac is cooking, put the egg yolk in a bowl. Blend in the mustard, vinegar and a pinch of salt. Beat in the olive oil, drop by drop at first, then in a thin stream as the mixture thickens. When all the oil has been incorporated, season to taste with salt and pepper. The mayonnaise should be highly flavoured.

Drain the celeriac. As soon as it is cool enough to handle, peel it and cut in into neat cubes.

Fold the warm celeriac, the ham, the carrots and parsley into the mayonnaise. Correct the seasoning if necessary. Serve very cold in a bowl lined with lettuce leaves.   **147**

SALSIFY GRATIN

SERVES FOUR TO SIX
2¹/₂ lb (1¹/₄ kg) salsify or scorzonera
Lemon juice
Salt
1 teaspoon sugar
1¹/₂ oz (45 g) butter
1 oz (30 g) flour
¹/₂ pint (250 ml) hot milk
¹/₄ chicken stock cube
2 egg yolks
1 oz (30 g) Gruyère or Emmenthal
  cheese, freshly grated

Scrape the salsify and cut them into 2-inch (5 cm) lengths, quickly dropping them into water acidulated with lemon juice to prevent them discolouring. Put the salsify in a pan of water, add salt and the sugar and bring to the boil. Simmer for 15 to 20 minutes, or until tender. Drain well.

Preheat the oven to 350°F (180°C, Gas Mark 4).

Melt the butter in a heavy saucepan. Blend in the flour and stir over a low heat for 1 minute. Gradually add the milk, beating vigorously to prevent lumps forming. Stir in the piece of stock cube. Bring the sauce to the boil and let it simmer gently, stirring occasionally, for 15 minutes. Remove the pan from the heat.

Beat the egg yolks lightly. Gradually beat a few tablespoons of the hot sauce into the yolks, then pour the mixture back into the pan. Flavour with a few drops of lemon juice and season to taste with salt.

Fold the salsify into the sauce. Pour the mixture into a *gratin* dish. Sprinkle with the cheese and bake for 15 minutes or until the salsify is heated through and the cheese on top has melted and begun to colour slightly.

SAUTÉED POTATOES WITH GARLIC

SERVES FOUR TO SIX
2 lb (1 kg) potatoes
3 tablespoons olive oil
3 plump garlic cloves, peeled
Coarse salt
Finely chopped parsley, to garnish

Peel the potatoes and cut them up into cubes
of about 1 inch (2 cm). Rinse the cubes in a
colander and dry them thoroughly with
kitchen paper.

In a large, deep frying-pan that has a lid
and will take the potatoes in a single layer,
heat the olive oil. Fry the garlic cloves slowly
until they are just golden. Add the potatoes
and fry them, tossing them constantly, over
moderate heat for 5 minutes, or until they
have coloured on all sides.

Sprinkle the potatoes with salt. Cover the
pan and fry the potatoes very slowly, shaking the pan and turning them occasionally,
for about 15 minutes, or until they are crisp
and golden brown on all sides and feel soft
inside when pierced with a fork.

Lift the potato cubes out of the pan with a
slotted spoon. Discard the garlic cloves.
Drain the potatoes thoroughly and serve
immediately, sprinkled with more salt and
garnished with parsley.

JANSSON'S TEMPTATION

Traditionally one of a selection of dishes in a *smörgasbord*, this famous Swedish potato and anchovy dish makes an excellent main dish for lunch or supper.

SERVES TWO AS A MAIN DISH,
FOUR AS AN APPETIZER
4 medium-sized potatoes
Butter
1 large Spanish onion, shredded
¼ pint (125 ml) single cream
¼ pint (125 ml) milk
Salt and pepper
2 oz (60 g) anchovy fillets, drained
4 tablespoons coarse white
breadcrumbs

Peel the potatoes and cut them into matchstick-sized strips.

Heat 1½ ounces (45 g) of butter in a deep frying-pan. Add the onions and fry them gently until they are soft and transparent, but not coloured. Mix in the potato sticks and fry them gently for 3 minutes, turning them to coat them with the butter. Stir in the cream and milk. Season to taste with salt and pepper (but bear in mind the saltiness of the anchovies to come) and simmer very gently for a few minutes longer so that the potatoes just begin to soften.

Preheat the oven to 400°F (200°C, Gas Mark 6).

Spread half of the potato and onion mixture over the bottom of a shallow baking dish. Arrange the anchovy fillets evenly over the top and cover with the remaining potatoes, onions and cream. Sprinkle with the breadcrumbs and dot with a few pieces of butter.

Bake the dish for 30 minutes, or until the potatoes feel tender when pierced with a skewer and the top is golden and bubbling.

Vegetable Fruits

Tomatoes, cucumbers, pumpkins, marrows, courgettes, aubergines and capsicums are all fruits which are almost always prepared and served as vegetables. They all originated in distant, sunny lands and were brought by travellers and explorers to Europe, where they became an integral part of many cuisines. Today it is almost impossible to imagine what cooks would do without them.

BAKED COURGETTES WITH EGGS AND CHEESE

SERVES FOUR
6 tablespoons olive oil
2 garlic cloves, crushed
1½ lb (¾ kg) courgettes, sliced
1 large mild onion, thinly sliced
2 tablespoons chopped parsley
1 teaspoon chopped basil
Salt and pepper
6 eggs
4 tablespoons single cream
3 oz (90 g) grated Gruyère cheese
1 oz (30 g) grated Parmesan cheese
1 tablespoon butter

Preheat the oven to 350°F (180°C, Gas Mark 4).

Heat the oil in a large, deep frying-pan. Add the garlic and fry gently, stirring, for 1 minute without letting it brown. Add the courgettes, increase the heat and fry, stirring frequently, until lightly browned. Stir in the onion and the herbs. Season to taste. Reduce the heat and cook, stirring occasionally, until the onions are soft. Tip the contents of the pan into a baking dish.

In a bowl, beat the eggs lightly with the cream, mix in the cheeses and pour over the courgettes. Dot with the butter and bake for 20 to 30 minutes, or until the eggs have set and the top is golden.

151

RECIPES

TOMATO TART

SERVES FOUR TO SIX
1½ lb (¾ kg) ripe, firm tomatoes,
   peeled
6 oz (180 g) puff pastry, made-up
   weight
3 oz (90 g) Gruyère or mild Cheddar
   cheese, grated
1 oz (30 g) softened butter
4 tablespoons double cream
2 eggs, lightly beaten
Salt and pepper

Preheat the oven to 450°F (230°C, Gas Mark 8). Put a heavy baking sheet in the oven to heat.

Cut each tomato into quarters and squeeze to remove the seeds. Chop the tomatoes and leave them to drain in a colander.

Roll the pastry out thinly and line a 9-inch (23 cm) fluted tart tin with a removable base. Sprinkle the pastry evenly with 1 ounce (30 g) of the grated cheese.

Work the remaining cheese to a fluffy paste with the butter and cream. Then beat in the eggs and season lightly with salt and pepper.

Season the chopped tomatoes and spread them evenly over the base of the pastry-lined tin. Spoon the egg and cheese mixture over the tomatoes.

Put the tart on the hot baking sheet in the oven. After the first 5 minutes, reduce the temperature to 400°F (200°C, Gas Mark 6); after another 5 minutes turn it down to 350°F (180°C, Gas Mark 4). Continue to bake the tart for 30 minutes longer, or until the filling is puffed and richly coloured and the pastry crisp and cooked through.

TOMATO RICE

SERVES FOUR TO SIX

2 oz (60 g) butter
1 lb (½ kg) ripe tomatoes, peeled and
    finely chopped
¼ teaspoon cayenne pepper
½ teaspoon sugar
Salt
1 large onion, sliced
½-inch (1 cm) piece fresh root ginger,
    peeled and finely chopped
1 garlic clove, crushed
¾ lb (360 g) long-grain (basmati)
    rice, washed, soaked in cold water
    for 30 minutes and drained

GARNISH
Chopped parsley
1 tablespoon chopped peanuts
2 hard-boiled eggs, quartered

Melt half the butter in a saucepan. Add the tomatoes, cayenne pepper, sugar and a little salt. Cook, stirring occasionally, for 10 minutes. Set aside.

Melt the remaining butter in a large saucepan. Add the onion, ginger and garlic and fry, stirring occasionally, over low heat until the onion is soft and golden.

Add the rice, increase the heat and fry, stirring, for 5 minutes. Pour in the tomatoes, season with more salt and add enough boiling water so that the liquid in the pan covers the rice by a ½ inch (1 cm). When the liquid boils rapidly, cover the pan, reduce the heat to very low and simmer for 20 minutes, or until the rice is cooked and all the liquid has been absorbed.

Spoon the rice into a heated serving bowl. Sprinkle the parsley and nuts on top and arrange the eggs decoratively around the sides. Serve immediately.

TUNA-STUFFED CUCUMBER

This dish may be served alone as an appetizer or as part of a selection of mixed *hors d'oeuvre*.

SERVES FOUR
1 large cucumber
Salt
7 oz (210 g) canned tuna fish,
    drained
1 oz (30 g) butter
1 oz (30 g) cream cheese
1 tablespoon chopped parsley
1 tablespoon chopped mixed fresh
    herbs
Black pepper
1 lemon, thinly sliced, to garnish

Peel the cucumber and cut it crosswise into 2-inch (5 cm) pieces. Drop the pieces into boiling salted water and cook gently for 8 minutes. Drain and refresh the cucumber pieces in cold water until they are firm again and cold. Scoop out and discard the seeds and pulp from the centre of each piece. Dry the pieces on kitchen paper. Mash the tuna fish with the butter and cream cheese to make a smooth paste. Blend in the herbs and season to taste with salt and pepper.

Stuff the cucumber pieces with this mixture and chill until firm. Cut each piece across into ½-inch (1 cm) slices and serve immediately.

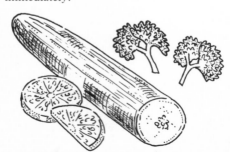

BAKED AUBERGINE

SERVES FOUR
3 lb (1 ½ kg) round aubergines
Salt
Olive oil
1 medium-sized onion, finely chopped
2 lb (1 kg) ripe tomatoes, peeled,
    seeded and chopped
3 sprigs fresh basil, chopped, or 2
    teaspoons dried basil
Black pepper
Flour
5 oz (150 g) Parmesan cheese, freshly
    grated
½ lb (¼ kg) Mozzarella cheese,
    thinly sliced
2 hard-boiled eggs, thinly sliced

Trim the stems from the aubergines. Cut the aubergines lengthwise into thick slices. Sprinkle each slice with salt. Put the slices in a colander and cover with a plate. Weight the plate down and leave the aubergines to drain for 30 minutes.

Heat 4 tablespoons of olive oil in a pan and fry the onion until golden. Add the tomatoes and basil, mix well and simmer gently, uncovered, until the tomatoes are reduced to a thick sauce. Season to taste.

Preheat the oven to 400°F (200°C, Gas Mark 6). Oil a large, shallow, ovenproof dish.

Rinse the aubergine slices in cold water. Pat dry and dust with flour. Fry in hot olive oil until soft and golden brown on both sides. Drain on kitchen paper.

Cover the bottom of the baking dish with a layer of aubergines. Sprinkle with Parmesan and cover with slices of Mozzarella and a few of hard-boiled egg. Spoon some of the tomato sauce over the top. Repeat these layers until the ingredients are used up, ending with tomato sauce. Bake for 30 minutes.

STUFFED PEPPERS

SERVES SIX
½ lb (¼ kg) short-grain rice
6 large green peppers
8 tablespoons olive oil
2 large, mild onions, finely chopped
3 oz (90 g) currants, washed
1 oz (oz (30 g) pine nuts
Salt and pepper
Sugar
6 tablespoons finely chopped parsley

Put the rice in a sieve and rinse thoroughly under cold running water. Pour a kettleful of boiling water over the rice and leave to drain for 1 hour.

Carefully cut out the stems of the peppers and set them aside. Scrape out the pith and cores. Rinse the peppers and leave them to drain, upside down, while the filling is prepared.

Heat the oil in a large fryingpan. Add the onions and fry, stirring, until they are transparent and a light golden colour. Stir in the rice, currants and pine nuts. Season to taste with salt, pepper and sugar. Continue to fry over moderate heat, stirring constantly, until the rice is golden. Stir in the parsley.

Fill the peppers with the rice mixture, leaving room for the rice to expand. Place the reserved stems on top.

Put the upright peppers close together in a heavy saucepan large enough to take them in one layer. Carefully pour in enough boiling water to come halfway up the sides of the peppers. Put the pan on the heat and bring water back to simmering point. Cover the pan, reduce the heat and cook the peppers very gently for 45 minutes to 1 hour, or until the rice is tender.

Allow the peppers to cool in the pan before removing them to a serving dish.
156 Serve chilled.

SOURED CREAM PUMPKIN PIE

SERVES SIX

*Shortcrust pastry made with 6 oz
    (180 g) flour*
1 lb (½ kg) pumpkin purée
½ pint (250 ml) soured cream
3 eggs, separated
¼ teaspoon salt
1 teaspoon ground cinnamon
½ teaspoon ground ginger
¼ teaspoon grated nutmeg
6 oz (180 g) castor sugar
Whipped cream

Preheat the oven to 425°F (220°C, Gas Mark 7).

Roll out the pastry and line a 9-inch (23 cm) tart tin. Prick the pastry all over with a fork. Line with greaseproof paper and fill with dried beans. Bake the pastry shell for 10 minutes. Remove the paper and beans and reset the oven to 350°F (180°C, Gas Mark 4). Return the pastry case to the oven for 10 to 15 minutes to dry out the base.

In a bowl, combine the pumpkin, soured cream and the lightly beaten egg yolks. Mix in the salt, spices and half the sugar. Place the bowl over gently simmering water and cook, stirring constantly, until thick.

Whip the egg whites until they form soft peaks. Gradually beat in the remaining sugar. Fold the meringue into the pumpkin mixture.

Spoon the pumpkin mixture into the pastry shell. Bake the pie for 45 minutes, or until the top is golden. Serve with the cream.

MARROW GRATIN

SERVES FOUR TO SIX
3 lb (1½ kg) marrow
Salt
2 tablespoons olive oil
2 oz (60 g) butter
1 large onion, coarsely chopped
2 large tomatoes, peeled and chopped
¼ lb (120 g) Cheddar cheese, grated
Black pepper

Cut the marrow into 1-inch (2 cm) slices. Peel the slices and remove the pith and seeds from the centre. Cut the marrow slices into 1-inch (2 cm) pieces. Put them in a colander, sprinkle with salt, toss well and leave to drain for 1 hour.

Preheat the oven to 375°F (190°C, Gas Mark 5).

Heat the oil and half of the butter in a large saucepan. Add the onion and fry, stirring occasionally, until soft and transparent. Add the tomatoes and simmer until reduced to a purée. Rinse the marrow chunks and add to the pan. Stir to mix. Cover the pan and simmer over low heat for 7 to 8 minutes. Stir in 1 ounce (30 g) of the grated cheese and season to taste with salt and pepper. Transfer the contents of the pan to a shallow baking dish. Sprinkle the remaining cheese on top and dot with the remaining butter. Bake for 30 minutes, or until tender and golden brown.

Entries in **bold** type refer to recipes

159

INDEX